# SALT FOR SOCIETY

# SALT FOR SOCIETY

## W. PHILLIP KELLER

**WORD BOOKS**
PUBLISHER
4800 WEST WACO DRIVE
WACO, TEXAS
76703

SALT FOR SOCIETY
Copyright © 1981 by W. Phillip Keller
All rights reserved. No portion of this book may be
reproduced in any form without the written permission of
the publisher. Unless otherwise indicated, all Scripture
quotations are from the authorized King James Version.

ISBN 0-8499-0290-8      ISBN 0-8499-3059-6/pbk
Library of Congress Catalog Card Number: 81-52379

67898 FG 987654321

*Printed in the United States of America*

To my Dad,
who was
*Salt for Society*

*A Word of Appreciation*

First to those many people who again and again have requested to have these studies put into book form.

Then to Mr. Richard Harris who taped the sessions and allowed me to use the tapes for reference purposes.

Finally to my wife, Ursula, who turned my rough, handwritten manuscript into an acceptable form the publishers could read.

# Contents

# Part I

## *Western Society Stricken with Terminal Illness*

# An Assessment

△

"Society is sick!" This statement is heard again and again. Often it is made with a shrug of the shoulders or a forlorn shake of the head. For some people it is a cause for genuine concern. To others it is simply a reason to be cynical about life in general.

For those of us who are a part of human society it is imperative to understand clearly what our dilemma really is. It is not good enough merely to hang our heads in despair over the decay of our civilization. We need to see what has gone wrong without giving way to the despondency and skepticism of modern man.

My reasons for saying this are straightforward. First of all our Heavenly Father has a great concern and love for human society. In the New Testament the word used to denote society is "The world." For example, "God so loved the world, that he gave his only begotten Son, that whosoever believeth in him should not perish, but have everlasting life" (John 3:16).

Or as our Lord prayed just before His death, "As thou hast sent me into the world [the society of men], even so have I also sent them into the world" (John 17:18).

He made it very clear that His followers were not to opt out of society. It was never His intention that they should withdraw from the company of their contemporaries. Rather He thrust them into the midst of men that they might act as His representatives.

Secondly there remains the eternal hope and optimism of our God. He will not permit darkness to overcome light. He will see to it that life prevails over death. And He assures us that His love can surpass our despair. In all of this divine activity we as His people are to be active agents.

He stated categorically that it is we who belong to Him, who are "The light of the world." He said also, "You are the salt of the earth." Yet most of us do not clearly grasp how that can be—probably because we do not truly realize the deepening darkness of the society in which we live, nor the illness of which we are an integral part.

After all, most of us who read this book are products of the Western world. We have been conditioned by our culture to conform to certain standards. In our sophistication we assume our culture is the most advanced and desirable ever to appear on the planet.

Perhaps we are wrong in all of this.

Perhaps we have been led to believe a lie.

Perhaps in ignorance we of the Western world have been deluded by false gods, yet knew them not.

In our pride as the most enlightened society on earth we have become stricken with a terminal illness. It appears to be benign when in truth it is malignant. What is it? Could it be our arrogance as a society?

## 1) Arrogance in Education

As a young boy, growing up in the tough, frontier environment of East Africa, I was constantly told that education was the key to success. Over and over I was told that an uneducated person simply had no hope to make a mark in the world.

I was part of a society which in the 1920s had only about 10 percent literacy. Fewer than 1 percent of our population would ever enter any college or university. So education was extolled as the panacea for all of our problems.

"Educate people!" was the cry heard everywhere. "Just civilize them!" was the theme of the day. "When men have understanding, learning and knowledge they will no longer become embroiled in conflict, wars and international intrigue."

These were empty promises. They were false hopes. In fact they became a counterfeit god.

We of the Western world have put enormous emphasis on education. Our educators have taken their message to the ends of the earth.

It is true there was a time when education was entrusted in large measure to the church. There was an era in our Western history when many of our great universities and colleges were Christian in character and conduct. But not so now.

Studies show that fewer than one half of 1 percent of the faculty on campuses are Christians. The net result is that higher education is in the hands of those who do not know God and choose deliberately to ignore Him.

Literally millions of students spend years and years acquiring knowledge without any reference to God or His important part in human history. Yet society insists that our educational systems are the finest devised by men.

## 2) Arrogance in Economics

As the so-called "Titillating '20s" passed into the "Terrible '30s" the whole world became engulfed in economic disaster. A depression that degraded and humiliated mankind ground people into abject poverty.

So the cry that arose was, "Let us find an economic solution!" Men turned to all sorts of "new deals." In some countries socialism was seen as the solution. In others capitalism was considered best.

It was assumed naïvely that economists could come up with solutions that would solve the awful unemployment, widespread hunger and terrifying specter of utter bankruptcy that confronted society.

Instead it was soon apparent that man's way out was to go to war. The very adversities of conflict, international intrigue and inhumanity of man to man which education was supposed to dispel now descended upon the earth in double fury.

In their hunger, arrogance and anger, men did not turn to God. They turned to guns. War would usher in an era of unparalleled prosperity and affluence. This artificial and spectacular demand for ships, planes, tanks, ammunition, arms and other military gear would reverse the deadly stagnation of the depression.

So in our arrogance, pride and pomp, as the world's most sophisticated societies, we have paraded our military might for the last forty years.

And though Western society has boasted of unparalleled affluence, by a strange irony its people have felt a deep disquiet. Somehow all of this enormous wealth could be wiped out overnight. The energy crisis confirms that conviction.

### 3) Arrogance in Politics

The "Furious '40s" were years which most people prefer to forget. The depths to which society sank in those diabolical days will probably never be fully plumbed.

The atrocities perpetrated by supposedly modern and enlightened peoples are almost too ghastly to recount: the wholesale extermination of Jews in Germany; the incredible torture of men and women in concentration camps; the total destruction of entire cities by massive bombings; the death of uncounted millions of innocent women and children; the fire bombings; the use of atom bombs; the sinking of merchant ships; the total devastation of magnificent farmland all remain as terrible insights into the utter depravity of human society.

So a shout went up from all over the scorched and battle-broken earth. "Give us peace—give us a political panacea—give us a safe solution to our sinister self-destruction."

Again men did not turn to God. They did not seek for solutions in God's Word. They did not humble themselves under the hand of God.

Instead they turned to schemes of their own devising. August bodies such as the United Nations, the North Atlantic Treaty Organization, The European Economic Community were formed with no respect or regard for God.

Peace pacts of one kind or another were concluded. International agreements for nonproliferation of arms were signed. But still society went on engaging in war after war. Arms build-up continued, until today the whole earth trembles beneath its burden of military hardware. Our proud political posturing has proven nothing but our utter insanity as a society.

## 4) Arrogance in Science

The "Fabulous '50s" were supposed to usher in a brand new era of bright hope for all the survivors of the holocaust. There was a veritable explosion of scientific knowledge. So rapid was the rate at which new data poured out of our research centers and lavish laboratories that no one person could possibly keep pace with all the latest discoveries in his or her discipline.

In its intellectual arrogance and academic sophistication the scientific community, of which I am a part, declared boldly that they had the answers to man's dilemma. "Give us enough men; give us enough money; give us enough research facilities; give us enough time—and we will come up with answers!"

It was a proud posture. It still prevails in much of the scientific community. God is totally ignored. He cannot be subjected to the scientific process. He cannot be measured, weighed, analyzed or determined by the faculty of our five fallible human senses. Therefore it follows He must not exist. So He can be quietly dismissed from the academic halls of higher human investigation.

Sad to say, science simply has not solved the dilemmas of our day. Instead it has only magnified them. In some areas of human endeavor it has contributed constructively to research in medicine, agriculture and ecology. But by the same measure it has complicated the lives of all of us with its increasing pollution of the planet, its destructive waste of natural resources, its endangering of the environment, its spawning of military gadgetry for mass murder.

No, our scientific arrogance in society is sinister and insidious beyond words to describe.

## 5) Arrogance in Sociology

As we moved into the "Sizzling '60s" a new cry arose in the Western world. We trumpeted from our television and radio towers that "a great new society" was about to emerge. There poured from our presses and people a floodtide of sophisticated information on how to heal the hurts of a suffering society.

A whole new generation of "war babies" was bursting onto the social scene. They were a generation determined to turn things around. They had none of the old inhibitions of their predecessors to humble their haughtiness. They knew nothing of privation in education. They had not been through a depression. The war years were but the nightmare memories of their parents. And science now stood ready to serve any selfish wish or whim of the human heart.

The upheavals, violence and fragmentation of family life were but symptoms of a society that felt free to abandon the heritage of its forefathers. Even within the church some were openly declaring with bellicose bravado, "God is dead." It was naïvely assumed that, by so speaking, fiction would become fact.

But God was not dead. In truth He was as much alive and active in the affairs of men and nations as ever before. Only men in their folly were repudiating the great godly heritage handed down to them. The Scriptures were scorned. A new form of morality was advocated. The main purpose of society was to establish new standards of behavior without reference to God's all-wise provision for man's proper conduct in society.

What utter folly and total self-deception!

## 6) Arrogance of Hedonism

Hedonism is best defined as the conduct of a society given to leisure, pleasure and treasure. It is in reality a heathen culture, predicated on the false premise that man is here only to luxuriate in his pleasure and affluence. It is essentially pagan and opposed to any control by God.

Basically this hedonistic life style has been the hallmark of Western society during the so-called "Soaring '70s." It has produced the "me" generation. This is the outlook of a people who assert vehemently, "If it feels good, it must be good."

This is a society given over to sensuality. The old philosophy of "eat, drink and be merry for tomorrow we die" is simply dressed up in a more sophisticated guise.

The common assumption is that each person is really a god unto himself. His main purpose for being upon the planet is simply to pander to his own pride, serve his own selfish interests, come under no authority to anyone else, much less God, and live with no sense of obligation or responsibility to another.

In a society with this philosophy God's interests are not even considered. Christ's edicts are not even regarded as relevant. Man is the ultimate achievement of the supposedly progressive evolutionary process. As such he need answer to no one for his conduct.

This is really humanism in its most reprobate form. It parades itself as the savior of mankind. It promises to set men free from any sort of servitude to the false idea of a living God.

Yet in so doing it enslaves men to the terrible tyranny of their own passions and perversion.

## 7) Arrogance of Christians

As we move into the "Awesome '80s" or the "dangerous decade," as it has been dubbed, we as Christians have to make a careful appraisal of our own position in society.

We must ask ourselves some searching questions.

Are we too tainted and tarnished by the conditioning of our own culture? We have been led to believe that ours is the finest, highest, most noble society produced in human history.

Are we proud of our achievements in education, economics, politics, science, sociology or humanism? Most of us have had to make our careers in one or other of these fields of human endeavor. Have we allowed human ideology, human philosophy, human values to superimpose themselves upon our way of thinking, our standard of behavior, our life style?

Is it true to say that we as Christians are an element in society that is as distinct as salt to food, or light to darkness? Or is the reverse true? Has society actually succeeded in impinging itself upon us to the extent we are no different than the world.

A great uneasiness is beginning to be felt amongst God's people everywhere. It is no longer a case where the church is vigorously penetrating the world with God's message of salvation. It is now a case of the world penetrating the church with humanistic philosophies, cultural pride, business techniques and contemporary conduct.

Because of this the church probably stands in its greatest hour of peril, despite its apparent popularity and prominence in Western society. For arrogance always comes before a terrible fall.

It is imperative, therefore, that we see clearly what our Lord said our role should be as *Salt for Society.*

# Part II

---

## *The Distinctives of a Christian in Society*

# 1

# *People Poor in Spirit*

△

We can turn to no higher authority than our Lord Himself for a definitive assessment of a Christian's character and conduct in society. He did not leave us in the dark as to what contribution His followers should make to their times and culture.

That is what this book is all about. It is intended to help us see and understand clearly what God looks for in His people. It endeavors to show that He is as much concerned with what we are in character as with what we do in our conduct.

We in Western society, in the occidental world, are very much preoccupied with "doing." Too often we assess a person's success based on his or her achievements. By contrast in the oriental world much more emphasis is placed upon "being." In other words, what sort of a person is one? It is asserted that if one's character and person are right and noble, then it will follow that one's attitudes and behavior will be correct and proper.

In short, what "I am" is more important than what "I do."

Our Lord put it this way: "Every good tree bringeth forth good fruit; but a corrupt tree bringeth forth evil fruit" (Matt. 7:17).

So, one day, shortly after He had set out on His public ministry, Jesus climbed a steep mountain slope taking His favorite followers with Him. Settling Himself amongst the boulders and brush on the summit, He began to instruct the young men around Him as to what it entailed to be one of His people.

Like younger folk of any generation and culture, they were eager and energetic. They were charged with dreams and hopes and enormous expectations for the future. They wanted to turn things around in their troubled times. Their little nation of Israel had been invaded and colonized by the iron-shod armies of the mighty Roman Empire. They were subject to severe taxation and tough imperial laws that ground them down in humbling servitude.

Casting their eyes across the broad plains and khaki-colored hills of their homeland they were sure they had found their long awaited *Messiah* in this One whom they called *Master.* In the blue haze that hung in the still air over their beloved Galilee, they sensed a deep stirring of their fiery spirits. What would Jesus say? What secrets would He share with them for future action? What strategy would He lay out that would enable them to unhinge the might of the cruel Caesars?

These young firebrands were prepared to die for the deliverance of Israel. It did not matter what it would take. They were determined to see a new kingdom set up in their generation. It might be through education, political intrigue, economic shifts of power, military might, or sociological changes. Whatever their leader, their teacher, their master, "Rabboni," said, they would do.

Eagerly, intensely, expectantly they hung on His words.

His very first sentence stunned them into silence. "Blessed are the poor in spirit: For theirs is the kingdom of heaven" (Matt. 5:3).

It just simply did not seem sensible.

After all wasn't it the person full of spirit, full of fire, full of ideas and inspiration who went out to set society on fire?

If we pause to think seriously about this matter, we, too, must confess that like so many things Jesus said this cuts diametrically across our ideas. It runs counter to all our cultural conditioning.

Proof that Jesus' disciples never fully fathomed this first basic concept of Christian character was their own subsequent conduct. James and John were nicknamed "the sons of thunder" so tempestuous were their tirades. All of the disciples, up to the very night of Christ's crucifixion, wrangled and fought and quarreled over prominence of place. Even Peter, probably the oldest of the lot, was prepared to carry a sword beneath his belt to bring in the kingdom of heaven. Several of the flaming young fellows would have called down fire of destruction on anyone who thwarted their plans.

No, poverty of spirit was a characteristic rather foreign to the fiery temperament of Jesus' associates. And it is very much the same with us.

From our babyhood, we in the West are urged to "Stand on your own feet"; "Make your own decisions"; "Reach for the top"; "Push your way ahead"; "Plan your work, then work your plan"; "Assert yourself"; "Fulfill yourself"; "Decide your own destiny."

So thoroughly and deeply are we thus conditioned by our culture that to be considered "poor in spirit" strikes us as being anything but successful.

What then did our Lord really mean?

First of all we must understand what God means when He uses the word "spirit."

In our contemporary, non-Christian society man is considered to be a dual being. He is said to have a body with its physical drives, desires and daily habits. He is also said to have personality . . . or, as some put it, "person." This personality is made up of his mind with its thought processes, his emotions with all of their feelings and sensations, and his volition, or will, with which decisions are made and aims maintained.

But beyond this God's revelation is that man is in fact a tripartite being. He does have a body with all its physical capacities. He does have a person with all of its soulish capacities of thought, emotion and volition. But beyond this he also possesses a spirit with its capacity to know God who is a Spirit; to see and understand God in a clear conscience; to have intimate and personal communion with God in spirit and truth.

God is a Spirit: and they that worship him [i.e. commune with him] must worship him in spirit and in truth (John 4:24).

It is in the area of our spirits that so many of us have real difficulty in our dealings with God. This is because in our society, in our education, in our science we have been taught that we can function without spiritual reference to God. In our pride and humanistic arrogance we have been led to believe that we can get along very readily without Him. He is totally ignored, by-passed and treated as if of no consequence.

Yet the truth is that the exact opposite is so. Until a person's spirit has been touched, made alive and energized by God's Spirit, he is truly dead in that area of life. And it is not until a person recognizes the poverty of his own spirit that there is any possibility of his coming to know God.

It is the proud person, the arrogant individual, the self-assured, self-satisfied soul who feels no need for God. This poses the perennial problem between God and man. It is the fundamental issue that underlies all other matters in our character and conduct.

It explains why Jesus mentioned it first.

If a man, deep in his spirit, did not sense a profound need for God; if he did not feel improverished, empty, unfulfilled; if in his spirit there was no void, no peculiar "pull," no deep inner ache for more than man could supply, the chances of becoming totally fulfilled would be minute indeed.

But happily for us the gracious, solicitous Spirit of our God does not leave us alone in our arrogant self-assurance. He does pursue us. He is "The Hound of Heaven." He is the Counselor who counsels us to seek and search for God. He is the One who tenderly, yet tenaciously turns us from our humanistic preoccupations to a longing for the living Lord. He is the Divine Suitor who woos our wandering spirits from the world to see the wonder of Christ's own superb character. It is He who shows us the indefatigable love of our Father God.

In all of His gracious and generous concern for us, we begin to discern, "Yes, indeed, I am poor in spirit. I am empty. I do need God. I am missing the mark in life. I must have this spiritual quickening of my spirit. I have to be aroused, awakened from my spiritual sleep. I must come alive to Christ, lest I die."

Such a person is blessed.

Such a person is favored.

Such a person is bound to find the reality, the very reason for all of life and the in-coming of God's kingdom—His presence and power in the everyday affairs of life.

Now in our day, just as in Jesus' day, people have real problems understanding the term "kingdom of God or kingdom of heaven."

Very briefly it can best be explained this way. It does not refer to the establishment of some unique, spiritual, earthly empire visible to our physical eyes or comprehended by our mortal minds.

The kingdom of heaven is the synonym for the government of God in a person's life. It is the quiet, inner control of our conduct by Christ the living Lord. It is to be subject in spirit to the supreme sovereignty of the Spirit of God.

Put another way, we can say that the person who is poor in spirit will capitulate to the call of God in Christ. Such people will surrender the sovereignty of themselves to the gracious Holy Spirit to be guided by Him. They will abdicate their role of self-control and self-realization to the supreme purposes of God. No longer will they be the "king in their own castles." Above all else, they will want to do only God's will and work in the world, no matter how attractive or tough it may be.

Now all of this is fairly simple to state on paper.

It is exceedingly difficult to experience in spirit.

For we are proud people.

We do not wish to be dictated to by another—not even God Himself.

Our preference is almost always to be our own bosses.

As long as this condition persists we are torn and fractured by inner conflicts. We are men and women of divided minds, divided loyalties, divided interests, divided decisions.

A Christian—Christ's person—cannot live that way.

If my character is to be consistent, if God is to govern me, if Christ is to condition my conduct, if the Spirit of God is to guide me, arrogance must go; pride must be pulverized and self-aggrandizment must end. I must become poor in spirit, humbled and contrite.

> The Lord is nigh unto them
> that are of a broken heart;
> and saveth such as be of
> a contrite spirit (Ps. 34:18).

How?

First, let it be said that if we ask God to humble us, He will take us seriously. The consequences may well be devastating and drastic. It is surprising just how suddenly wealth, health, position, prestige, success and friends can fade and fall away.

This is why we are exhorted to humble ourselves under the mighty hand of God. Read James 4:4–10.

There are several simple steps one can take:

1) Think much about the greatness of God. Take time each day to meditate quietly on His majesty and might displayed throughout the universe. Compare your own minuteness and fallibility.

2) Give your Father genuine gratitude for all the wondrous gifts, benefits, blessings bestowed on you. Name them. Recall them. Remind your proud spirit they all come from Him.

3) Concentrate on the consistency of Christ. See how patient, faithful and understanding He has been with you despite your perverseness and pride.

4) Quietly, sincerely, soberly contemplate the cost of Calvary for your redemption. The price for your total forgiveness and acceptance by God is beyond measure.

5) Consider the remarkable generosity of God in not only reconciling you to Himself by His own laid-down life, but also recognizing you as His dear child.

6) Run over in retrospect the supernatural ways in which God's Spirit has pursued you all the days of your life, down all the tangled trails of your wayward wanderings.

7) Contemplate in awe and wonder the remarkable selflessness of a living God who always acts only in your own best interests, who brings even the best out of your mistakes.

If you do these things, you will become poor and humble in spirit but rich in the presence and power of God.

His life will become your life. His wishes will become your wishes. His work will become your work in society. And you will become one who goes out to turn the world upside down because He is in you. Read Philippians 2:12–16.

# 2

# *Men and Women Who Mourn*

△

Who wants to mourn anyway?

All of the trends in our hedonistic society move in exactly the opposite direction. The emphasis of our times is to "Live it up"—"Laugh it off."

Most men and women choose to put on a bold, brave front that scoffs at the seriousness of death. They act as if "dying" is something that happens to other people but not to them. In many circles everything possible is done to minimize the impact of death. People are shielded from it by the sophisticated professionalism of modern science, modern medicine, modern morticians and the elaborate funeral arrangements which our culture has come to demand in the presence of death.

Dying and mourning and all the grief that attend the termination of life are subjects seldom discussed. We try to push them aside. We prefer to change the subject. We would rather not think about them at all.

But Jesus did.

He even went so far as to insist that the person who mourns is fortunate. Somehow He was sure that anyone who mourns is the recipient of a special and unusual benefit from above. In fact, He went even further to state that this individual, if indeed a follower of Christ, would experience comfort.

There are three distinct ways in which this happens—physical death, spiritual death, and suffering on behalf of others.

First there is the basic fact that for God's people, death is not the dreaded specter of the grim old reaper who comes to cut us down with his sinister scythe. For the Christian, death is the door through which we step into the personal presence of our living Lord. As it swings shut behind us, it closes off the chapter of our brief earth journey. Yet at the same instant it ushers us into the sublime dimension of a new life with our Father.

This was brought home to me in a most wondrous way during the death of my first wife. We had both known for many weeks that the time of her "call to go home" was at hand. Carefully, together, in calmness of spirit we had surveyed all of the Scriptures that dealt with death. We were fully aware of all the remarkable revelations given to men by our Father as to what life would be like in His realm prepared for His people. All of this has been carefully recorded in my book *A Layman Looks at the Lord's Prayer.*

So as the hour of her departure approached, we sat side by side, hand in hand, quietly resting in the presence of Christ. His assurances to us that all was well enfolded us both in a spirit of peace and quiet acceptance that this was His arrangement.

Softly, in syllables barely audible she turned to me and breathed her last words: "Faithful, even unto death!" Then in that instant her spirit was gone.

A surge of moving air swept through the room. A brightness of light filled the atmosphere. The door that had stood open swung shut. And in that moment angel spirits sent from our Father swept her spirit away into the joyous presence of the One who loves us with an everlasting love.

From that day forward, though I mourned deeply, grieved by the departure of my beloved, I was comforted and consoled by the living presence of the gracious Spirit of God in a manner no human being could match. In my fierce bereavement there was given to me by God the oil of His own joy for the spirit of my heaviness and heartache.

It was during those days of dark loneliness, in the shadow of my sorrow, that Christ became to me more real, more living, more present than ever before. He, and He alone, comforted my soul beyond my ability to tell.

In all of that experience the words of the Master were totally authentic, absolutely true, utterly trustworthy.

But beyond this aspect of physical death, our Lord without doubt also had in mind the whole matter of spiritual death. It, too, is a subject which many shun—perhaps because it is even less understood than bodily death.

Spiritual death is to be separated, cut off from God our Father. It is to be in that condition where there really is no correspondence between Him and us. It is to be alive physically and morally, yet unaware of His presence or power which can impart a new dimension of life to us in the realm of our spirits.

Writing to the early Christians of his era, Paul reminded them repeatedly that they had previously been "dead." Read Ephesians 2:1–10 and Colossians 2:13–15.

But through the faithfulness of God Himself, who entreated them by His Spirit, they had been made alive, quickened and brought into communion with Christ.

However, this could only happen if first they had mourned over their spiritual death. Here is how that happens.

It is God's Spirit who comes to us, touching us in our spirits, *convicting us* that somehow there is a dimension in our lives where we are simply not alive. With a deep disquiet we sense that we are not in active communion with our Creator. There is something amiss. We are separated from

Him by a barrier of unbelief or even outright animosity or alienation.

If we are sincere and searching people, in quest of ultimate truth, this "undone" condition deep within our spirits will cause us deep despair. We will know, as the British put it, that something is "seriously out of joint." And our anguish of spirit will *convince us beyond question* that something has to be put right between us and God. Seeing ourselves undone before Him, we will confess our dead and lost condition. We, in fact, mourn our plight.

This is the person who, brought to this point by the faithful inner working of Christ's Spirit, finally flings himself on God's grace and cries out, *"O God, be merciful to me a sinner!"*

Such a one is blessed. Such a one is well on the road to reconciliation with God his Father. Such a one is on the path to peace with Christ.

For it is to this person that God's Own Spirit speaks immeasurable comfort and consolation. "You are forgiven. You are cleansed. You are justified. You are set free from your sins. You are accepted into the family of God."

All of these blessed benefits come only because, at some point, there has been a deep and genuine contrition of spirit to the point of mourning. The searching, yearning spirit deeply convicted of its undone condition, convinced of its need to be made alive to God, longing for acceptance, finds itself fulfilled in the wondrous generosity and loving kindness of a gracious Heavenly Father.

But, incredible as it may sound at first, God does even more than all this. He actually goes on to share our lives with us as a constant *Companion,* a *Comrade,* a *Counselor* by our side. Thus as we walk through life, we are continually assured of the *Comfort of His companionship.*

Let me put it another way.

The person poor in spirit, who in a spiritual dimension mourns and grieves over his or her own spiritual poverty, will best know the life of Christ made real within. It is the one who decries his own inner deadness who will most surely be made alive with the quickening assurance and comforting presence of God Himself.

As I pen these lines, there sweeps through my spirit again the acute and painful agony of those days in my life when I realized that in truth I was "dead to God." All my life I had listened to the Word of God. For almost forty years I had been attending all sorts of churches. Yet deep down in my spirit there was no acute awareness of the living Christ.

Graciously, persistently, patiently God's Spirit entreated me to turn from my self-assured, self-centered, self-confident conduct to seek Him. Oh, the turmoil of those times! Oh, the tears of anguish that flowed in the darkness of my despair! Oh, the melancholy mourning of a man who longed and yearned for God to quicken and make him alive in a new dimension of deliverance from death to life, from darkness to light, from despair to love.

And God did! Bless His name!

He is faithful.

He is true to Himself.

"Blessed are they that mourn for they shall be comforted!" God keeps His promises. He will give us new life. But first we must mourn our spiritual death.

In passing it must be stated here that this emphasis upon deep remorse and mourning over sin and selfishness in our lives is a note seldom emphasized in the modern church. Too often congregations are led to believe that Christianity is simply a case of accommodating one's self to some creed or dogma. Not so! The person who is ultimately to become salt in society or light in the world is one who at some point has mourned over the sins and selfishness that separate him from God. Read Isaiah 59.

This is the individual who discovers the amazing deliverance of God from the web of woe and wrong in which he has been enmeshed. This is the person who comes to know the living presence of the living Christ in his daily experience. This is the child of God in whom God's Spirit works to achieve His purposes upon the planet.

Mourning over our sins and selfishness then leads naturally to the third way in which Jesus meant that those who mourned would be comforted. It is a way that has to do with the grief and suffering God's people sense as they live and move in a society stricken with terminal illness.

Only the man or woman delivered from death to life can appreciate the peril of his or her contemporaries perishing all around.

Positive proof that there are literally thousands of so-called "Christians" who really are not yet alive to God is their total indifference to the dead and dying all around them. The dead do not mourn for the dead. It is the living who do. It is the ones alive to the dilemma of the dying who weep and wail. It is the living who travail in tears for the restoration and resurrection of the dead.

Ask yourself a few searching questions:

"When was the last time I wept for someone in sin?"

"When did I literally groan in grief over a world gone wrong?"

"When did my spirit literally sob in sorrow for a society of men and women streaming down the broad road of self-destruction?"

My father and mother were simple, sincere lay people, who felt the special call of God to pour out their lives for Africa and its pagan people. Many of my most vivid boyhood memories are bound up with the acute anguish of spirit and suffering of soul which they both endured on behalf of their beloved Africans.

Dad spent twenty-eight years in one of the most malaria-ridden areas of the continent, taking only two brief furloughs in all that time. He literally poured out every ounce of strength he possessed for his adopted people. He literally laid down his own brave life for the dying all around him.

He literally wept, pleaded and entreated thousands to turn from death to life.

Mother was no less devoted. She had an old rocking chair before which she kneeled for hours at a stretch, crying out to God for the tribespeople around her sunk in sin and death. The pillow on that old chair was soaked in tears again and again as she groaned and agonized over the decadence of the society in which she and Dad lived and worked.

We don't hear much about that sort of "mourning," that sort of grief, that sort of suffering today.

But God heard those heart cries. He respected that deep remorse. He was sensitive to the impassioned sincerity of those simple spirits.

He touched literally thousands and thousands of Africans. His gracious Spirit swept across the hills and valleys of that country convicting men and women in their homes, their fields, their marketplaces. People poured into the churches to find Christ and to find a new life in God.

In very truth that ancient passage from the Psalms came into living reality:

"They that sow in tears shall reap in joy" (Ps. 126:5).

Yes, they were comforted!

They knew the consolation of our God.

They sensed the comradeship of Christ in the church.

We live in a dying world amid a sick society. The darkness of despair deepens around us.

Yet there is given to us the great honor of being identified with our Master in His suffering for the world. He, too, looked out with anguish upon the culture of His times. He was moved to tears over the intransigence of His contemporaries. He felt enormous compassion for the lost and dying all about Him. Read Matthew 9:35–38.

He invites us, as His followers, to be caught up with Him in suffering for society. It is not enough to just look on objectively. He asks us to mourn with those who mourn, to weep with those who weep, to rejoice with those who rejoice. After the darkness comes the brightness of the dawn.

# 3

# *Those Who Inherit the Earth*

△

The third statement Jesus made about the character of a Christian is perhaps the most baffling of all. Not only did it dismay His tough young followers then, but also many of us today, especially men, who long to be His companions.

"Blessed are the meek, for they shall inherit the earth" may sound sweet and appealing to a mild-mannered person. But it is hardly the sort of statement to stir the spirit of our hard driving age. We of the West are not a passive people prepared to sit around waiting to inherit the earth.

Our philosophy is rather: "If you want it, you work for it!" "You struggle, scramble and strive to succeed!" "You fight to reach the top!"

As a young, rough, tough youth such prayers as: "Gentle Jesus, meek and mild, listen to a little child . . ." came within a hair's breadth of turning me away from the Master. I simply was not interested in One who was either mild or meek.

This unfortunate and untrue caricature of Christ across the centuries has done enormous damage to His reputation.

It explains why in so many places a much greater number of women rather than men follow Him. Most men are looking for a leader who appeals with his strength, his forcefulness, his ability to perform.

So we are bound to ask—What really did our Lord mean by the phrase, "The meek are fortunate and well favored"?

The answer will surprise most of us, simply because our understanding of the term *meek* is faulty. This word is used by Jesus both here and in Matthew 11:28–30:

> Come unto me, all ye that labour
> and are heavy laden,
> and I will give you rest.
> Take my yoke upon you,
> and learn of me;
> for I am meek and lowly in heart:
> and ye shall find rest unto your souls.
> For my yoke is easy, and my burden
> is light.

It simply does not mean to be weak, mild or insipid.

It has to do with very tough training, a severe discipline for service, an element of learning to handle heavy loads in the lightest way possible.

Jesus gave us this view clearly when He stated emphatically, "Take my yoke upon you and learn of me: for I am meek and lowly in heart."

Most of us in the twentieth century simply fail to comprehend what He had in mind. Let me explain.

Where I grew up as a lad in the frontier bush country of Kenya, almost all the transportation of goods and the breaking of new land was done by oxen. In my earliest boyhood memories, the training and breaking of massive, untamed Brahman bulls and bullocks were part of the wild excitement of taming the frontier.

In those distant days there were no tractors on our land.

There were no trucks on our rocky roads. There were only tough, powerful, straining teams of oxen that turned the rocky soil into fertile fields. There were only long spans of strong-muscled beasts that hauled great loaded wagons across the tough terrain.

We had no horses. Under our rigorous tropical climatic conditions horses simply succumbed and died. The only beasts strong enough, tough enough, sturdy enough to survive were the wild, hot-blooded, fierce-tempered Brahman bulls and bullocks.

My father kept a steady stable of about twenty-eight of these oxen. He owned some of the finest wagons, plows and farm equipment in Kenya. He was the first to import the most advanced ox-drawn equipment into East Africa.

All over the country he was known to have the most concern of any man for the welfare of his work oxen. His ox drivers were famous for the way in which they could get their oxen to haul enormous loads and perform veritable miracles in bringing the land into high production.

But the secret to all of this was bound up in "the breaking of the bulls and bullocks." These would come into my father's care as wild, snorting, furious beasts that had never had a yoke on their necks nor felt a chain binding them to a wagon or plow.

For the first weeks they would fight, bellow, paw the ground, roll in the dust and do all in their power to throw off the yoke. In anger, terror and blind fury they would fight to free themselves. It was a wild spectacle, often viewed with enormous excitement from the safety of a nearby tree where I would climb for a better view.

This whole fierce contest between master and bullock would gradually end in the big, raw-boned powerful bull being broken to bear the yoke and haul the great loads with steady purpose and quiet strength.

Any of the oxen that came into my father's care were the most fortunate in all the country. They were never overloaded. They were not allowed to be beaten or lashed with whips. They were given frequent rests on the road. If the weather was hot, they would work only under moonlight. They were fed the finest rations. They flourished and became intensely fond of their owner.

Yet all of this was because they were "broken" to serve. They were "broken" to the yoke. They were "broken" to use their enormous strength productively.

So essentially in the Scriptures where we find such phrases as: "broken-hearted"; "contrite in spirit"; "meek and lowly in heart"; this is what is meant. A man's will has been brought into subjection to the will of God. A person's powerful passions and drives and energy have been harnessed to do God's work in the world. The "meek" man is the disciplined man, trained and taught to take on great responsibilities and to discharge them without fuss and fanfare. He handles tough assignments with apparent ease.

The "meek" person is the one easily entreated of God. The Master need only speak the word and the worker will throw all of his full weight and strength into the enterprise. The "meek" man is the one under divine discipline who responds to the call of Christ and tackles the tough task without hesitation. The "meek" individual is the one who gets God's work done in the world without a lot of showmanship or theatrics.

He is the person who has "learned" that Christ's way to take life is by far the best. He no longer fights furiously to be freed from discipline. He does not try to assert his rights, struggle for supremacy and so wear himself out in warring with others.

It takes some of us a long time to discover the validity of this approach to life. Many of us, men especially, are a stiff-necked, stubborn lot. We will not bend or yield to another, be it God or man. We set our wills as fiercely as any Brahman bull. We believe somehow that the only sure road to success is to shatter any restraints put upon us. If necessary, we will smash the yoke, gore the driver or our fellow worker and set ourselves free from any discipline.

That is exactly the opposite to being meek and lowly in heart.

Are we surprised then that such individuals are those with no rest or repose? Are we surprised that these are the people for whom life really is a turmoil and sore trial? Are we surprised that these are the people driven to death by the fever and frenzy of their frustrations? Life for them, as Jesus said, was a straightforward case of being a real drag, a burden beyond their ability to bear.

But the one "broken" to the Master's yoke is the one who at last has stepped into stride with God. He acknowledges that Christ is in control. He accepts the load laid on him as matched to his strength. He admits that all is well and finds ease and rest therein.

The Master stated without hesitation that it was these who would inherit the earth. Of course most of us do not really believe this. Everything in our civilized culture cries out against such a concept. We who have been totally conditioned by our sophisticated Western society are sure that to be big, bold, brash and brazen is still best. We insist that one must simply get ahead on his own by grim determination and fierce fighting.

But for those few who may be disposed to agree with God let me list seven ways in which the meek do inherit the earth. Please note, Jesus did not say, "Earn the earth."

1) It is the meek person who finds that faith in God begins to flourish in his/her life. The self-made, self-sufficient individual sees no need to trust another, let alone Christ, as his Master.

But the man and woman broken to serve Christ come quickly to the place where they must trust Him for guidance and supervision and the supply of all their needs.

It is no longer a case of carrying on in one's own way. It is not a matter of doing one's own thing. It is not a question of realizing only one's own ambitions. Instead, life is seen from God's perspective. And to achieve the grand purposes of God, simple trust and quiet faith are needed. These He bestows in ample abundance upon the meek. And great results take place.

2) It is the meek person who discovers with great delight that God loves to draw near to the contrite and broken in spirit.

It is the man humble in will, obedient to the overtures of God's Spirit, who becomes acutely aware of God's presence. And though he himself may be of the earth, his sojourn here is rich and replete with the gracious companionship of Christ.

Even though he may be poor in material possessions, his inheritance in the constant comradeship of God can enrich his earthly days beyond human ability to express.

3) The meek man inherits a happy relationship with other people. Just as he can be entreated of God, so likewise he can be appealed to by his contemporaries. He does not sit up alone and aloof on his little pedestal of self-importance.

The meek people are the approachable people, the self-giving people, the self-effacing people. Their warmth, their compatibility, their cooperative attitude win the hearts of a hundred friends.

Their rich inheritance is the open entrance which they enjoy into scores of hearts and homes during their short earthly sojourn.

4) It is the meek who have learned to take time to "enjoy the flowers that grow alongside the path." They are not so "driven," so intent on attaining only their own ends in life, so ambitious for their own self-aggrandizement that they miss the magic of the moment.

Some of us see only the ultimate end upon which we have set our sights. We rush through life oblivious to the natural beauties about us. In our frenzy we forget to notice the fragrance of the fine things that adorn life's path. It is the meek who pause a moment here and there to be enriched by the bounties of the earth.

5) In our Western world we place too much emphasis upon attaining, achievements, ambitions. We are overly concerned and preoccupied with motivation. Somehow we must make our mark.

In this inner intensity we deprive ourselves of the special delight to be found in the actual process of achieving.

So much of our enterprise, rather than being a labor of love, becomes a burden to endure. We do not "relish the moment." We do not find pleasure in our work.

But the meek man does. Though he toils, it is with a twinkle in his eye, a whistle on his lips, a tune in his spirit. For he is inheriting the earth. His service is a joy and not a penance.

6) The meek individual has found the place of peace. He no longer struggles and fights and pushes to become top man on the totem pole of society. The threat of being pushed off his little pinnacle of prestige no longer haunts him.

He is not caught up in the pettiness of the so-called "pecking order." Content to quietly serve others, he has no fear of falling. There is no need to try so desperately to impress others. His main concern is to do whatever he does to the very best of his ability to satisfy the Master and thus bring Him honor.

So for him, the earth, instead of being a battle ground, becomes a happy home for the few years he is here. He is at peace with God, with others, with himself. And this indeed is a joyous inheritance.

7) Lastly the meek have a rich inheritance in the earth of quiet contentment. It is enough to belong to the Master. It is an honor to be in His service. It is sufficient to be used of Him to bless God and uplift others.

Whatever talents, strength, energy, ability or gifts God

may have bestowed, the meek use them all to serve their generation. Working with God in His purposes upon the planet, they find fulfillment in His wishes for them. In this way our Father's will is done on earth, that they see, that they relish, that they inherit with quiet contentment as God's yokefellows!

# 4

# *Men and Women Who Long for the Fullness of God*

△

When Christ made the categorical statement, "Blessed are they which do hunger and thirst after righteousness [after the very life of God Himself]: for they shall be filled," He was extending to us mortals one of the most far-reaching of all His commitments.

This is one of His most precious promises to the sons of men. It is one of the greatest guarantees of godliness given to us anywhere in God's Word. It is the absolute assurance of sharing His life even while living in the society of men.

Any who find in these life-giving words enormous inspiration, uplifting hope and strong reassurance can be sure they are Christians.

During those dreary years of my own life, which I sometimes refer to as "wilderness years" wherein I hungered, longed and yearned to know God in a real and intimate dimension, this verse came to me as a last hope of help. I clung to it tenaciously like a small refugee child clutching his last crust of bread. It was my hope for survival, my last means of finding help, my assurance that my spiritual hunger would be satisfied, my thirst for God quenched.

The words *hunger* and *thirst* as used by Jesus bear special significance. They parallel the plight of people in desperate despair. They depict the dire dilemma of men and women who are literally starving to death for lack of food or drink. They convey the picture of people underfed, undernourished, who long for life-giving sustenance.

We in Western society know little of such extreme need. We see films showing the atrocious conditions prevailing in other parts of the world where untold thousands die from famine. We read heart-rending accounts of terrible privation in our newspapers and magazines. Yet few of us have lived or worked among the dead and dying who succumb from malnutrition. Because of our own affluence, government support agencies, and relative abundance of food and drink, we know little of the cruel symptoms of starvation.

However, as a young man, I knew what it was to go day after dreadful day without enough to eat. I knew the fierce, gnawing, convulsive spasms of a killing hunger that could not be assuaged. I would go into the bush and actually eat the green bark from certain shrubs that I felt somehow would at least fill my stomach and tide me over the torment of my hunger.

This is totally different from the pleasant hunger-pangs that precede a delicious dinner. Likewise, the awful burning thirst of the man in the desert about to die beneath the burning sun is far removed from the titillating thirst of the person who is teased by the sweet aroma of another cup of coffee.

In the one instance it is a case of give me food, give me drink or I die. In the other it is merely a matter of indulging a daily habit. And here it must be said that it is not until the spirit of a man or woman yearns earnestly, intensely, fiercely for the very life-giving Spirit of God, that he/she really understands what Jesus meant.

This hungering and thirsting takes many forms. People all through human history have tried in various ways to satisfy it. In fact men will try almost everything under the sun for fulfillment. They will turn to any tantalizing fare that holds out hope, some very deceptive. They will drink from any source, no matter how polluted, to try and appease their inner emptiness.

We are deluded by our society and culture to believe that we can be complete people by education, economics, sociology or any other of the popular panaceas offered to us. But men and women still go on hungering, thirsting, yearning for something beyond human ability or ingenuity to satisfy.

I was one of those. I tried athletics. I tasted all sorts of adventure. I climbed mountains. I photographed lions, elephants, buffalo, elk, mountain sheep, grizzly bears. I owned beautiful ranches. I bred the finest sheep and cattle on the continent. I made radio and television appearances. I threw myself into the conservation cause and lectured all over the country. I helped establish national parks. I wrote books. I served as a journalist roving the world. I made friends far and wide. I traveled to some forty or more countries. I enjoyed recognition in various fields of endeavor . . . but still I panted for that fulfillment which only God Himself could give.

In spite of the human contention that man is no more than a body and mind, the unique revelation given to us in God's Word by God's Spirit is that man, too, is a spirit. And not until our spirits become vitalized by communion with God's own gracious Spirit do we ever know this essential "filling" of our spiritual void that makes us whole.

Just as my body must have food and drink from a source outside itself to survive, so my spirit must be sustained from a source outside itself to thrive. That source is Christ Himself . . . it is essentially His life, His presence, and His power being imparted to me.

This life of His, this so called "righteousness" of God, comes to me in two remarkable ways.

First it comes through the astonishing generosity of God's own character and conduct toward me. He it is who in His own compassion for my great need of Him has come into human society and acted on my behalf.

He, the living God, in the guise of a man, Jesus the Christ, was born, lived, grew up, worked, was crucified, and rose from the grave among us, He ascended back to His splendor among us.

In all of this, though subject to the strains and stresses of our human society, he never sinned. His was a perfect performance. His was a life without a single stain. His was the "perfect doing" and "perfect dying" required to redeem all men for all time from all their wrongs and sins and stains.

Read 2 Corinthians 5:14–21 carefully.

It was in my stead He did all this: He paid the penalty for all my wrongs. He bled and suffered and died for me. He took my sins to set me free. It was to satisfy His own righteousness that He became my substitute. He did this to impute to me His own wondrous righteousness.

This is a titanic transaction of eternal dimensions. God, very God, in Christ takes my sins and gives me His goodness . . . His own righteousness.

Nothing else can satisfy my searching spirit. I look away from myself to see the splendor of His supreme self-sacrifice for my salvation. I see that He has made me whole. He has enfolded and filled me with His righteousness. He has accepted me as His own son. He is my living Lord and Savior. He is my Father!

My spirit leaps for joy, where before it was sunk with sin and despair. His Spirit bears witness with my spirit that I am now His son. In overwhelming appreciation and gratitude, I look up and my spirit cries, " 'Abba Father!' O God, You are my Father. You have loved me with infinite love.

You have quickened me, touched me, made me alive to Yourself!" And my longing is satisfied.

In this way I come to Christ, I partake of God Himself (the Bread of Life), never to hunger again. For He totally satisfies the yearning of my soul.

All of the great achievements accomplished for me by Christ in the context of history, I claim by faith. I look away objectively and see that His perfect provision for me is the entire basis upon which I stand now acquitted, justified and accepted in His family.

My personal, private response to His generosity is an act of living faith. From the depths of my spirit there wells up a springing, overflowing stream of gratitude to God for His enormous generosity to me.

I have partaken of His life. I have been satisfied with His remarkable redemptive kindness. I am literally re-made, re-created, re-charged, re-born by His gracious goodness to me as a man. None of it is earned. None of it is merited. None of it is deserved.

Freely, fully, there flows to me the very righteousness of God. It is imparted to me (credited to me without charge) and I stand stricken, overwhelmed and ecstatic with appreciation for His loving-kindness. My sins are swept away, forgiven, forgotten in the immensity of His generosity.

This is all of God.

This is a measure of His magnificence.

This is the essence of His very character.

In adoring gratitude I open my whole life to His in-coming. I eagerly invite Him to share my days, my experience, my very spirit.

But there is beyond all this a sublime, wondrous, intimate dimension in which God satisfies my questing spirit. He actually does deign to come now and reside with me in person.

This, too, is an act of faith. This is a personal, private

response on my part to Himself. He is no longer just a historical Jesus. He is no longer a distant deity. He is no longer some obscure spirit. I actually drink of His divinity.

He actually comes into my spirit by His Spirit to reside. He is the living Christ who, very much alive, arises to become the dominant person in my experience. He fills my life.

This "filling" by God's Spirit of which Jesus spoke and about which much has been said in the New Testament appears to confuse many. It really need not to be so if we understand in simple terms what is meant.

To be filled with the presence of God is to enjoy His company and companionship in all of life. It is to know Him as our life mate, exactly as in a beautiful marriage. Two people never really "know" each other until they become fully open and available to each other. It is only when each has invited the other to come into his or her life and fully share all their experience that their days are "filled" with the other's presence and person.

This is why Jesus referred to Himself as the groom, and His Church (you and me) as His bride. He comes into our lives to fill them continuously with His own person, His own presence, His own influence.

It is this acute, constant, exquisite awareness of God's presence that leads us to say, "O God, You are here in all Your plenitude. O Christ, You are here in all Your compassion and care. O gracious Spirit, You are here in all Your gentle graciousness to guide, lead and direct my every decision all the days of my life."

To open my life to God is to have my life filled with the life of God. It is to know the constant in-coming of Christ in every detail of my conduct. It is to experience the total satisfaction of knowing God's Spirit imparting Himself to my spirit.

The whole nub of the question as to whether or not I am totally filled with the life of God is not a matter of my getting more of Him, but rather the practical reality of Him getting more of me.

Most of our lives are so crowded and clogged with the clutter of our culture and social conditioning that there is little room for the fullness of His life to spring up in us with power.

I was reminded of this years ago when I purchased a dilapidated and neglected mountain ranch. The old owner took me down to where he said a beautiful spring of water once flowed beneath a great mountain outcrop. Now only an insipid little seep of muddy water came out of a conglomeration of dense brush, old rotted fences and fallen rock.

I decided to see if the spring could be restored. It took enormous work to clear out all the wild brush, brambles, nettles and rank growth that had choked the spring. Then there was the accumulated debris of leaves, twigs and rotten wood that had fallen into the flow. Finally the mud and earth and rocks and dung that livestock had trampled into the spring for years had to be cleared away.

As I worked on the spot, the water began to flow more and more fully. The sparkle returned as the spring began to bubble up again with new vitality. Gradually it swept away the last vestiges of dirt and debris. And where before there had been only a murky mud hole there now sparkled a shining basin of beautiful mountain water overflowing with a powerful stream of crystal clear refreshment. A place of despair had become a spot of rare beauty and great delight. Often, after that, we would go there to picnic and refresh ourselves from the delicious flow.

This is exactly what Christ promised could actually happen in a person's life.

Read John 4:1–26 and John 7:37–40.

Our lives can be flowing with the continuous fullness of God. They can be the source of refreshing to others. They can be an oasis of life in a sick society.

But we must want this to happen. We must yearn for

God. Be careful what you want from God! You get what you hunger and thirst for in sincerity.

If you *want* to be filled, then the folly and foolishness of the old life style must go. Then God comes in with all His beauty and power. If you don't really care, it will never happen.

# 5

# *Those Marked by Mercy*

△

Earlier in this book it was stated that the person who is to make an impact for God in our hedonistic society must be different from it. Such people must have unusual and unique qualities of character which distinguish them from their fellows. These attributes are not peculiarities which we try to portray by rigid regimentation of our behavior. Rather they are the glad, irrepressible, spontaneous springing-up of the life of Christ within us.

The fresh, crystal, sparkling water that bubbles up from a spring does not originate with the spring. It has as its source the distant snow-mantled mountains where the snow or rain first fell. The spring is but the spot where that perennial flow of refreshing underground water comes to the surface. There it bursts into view to refresh all those who drink from it.

So with our lives, the source of our spiritual life lies in the grandeur and splendor of the gracious Spirit of our God. The refreshment, inspiration and impact of that divine life can find full expression if allowed to do so through our little lives. Others who touch us can in truth tell that the source of our blessing and benefit to our generation lies not with us, but beyond, with Christ Himself.

The true mark of the man and woman in whom God's life flows freely is their innocence of their own inspiration. There is a beautiful, relaxed, quiet gentleness about the personality permeated by God's Spirit. One of the most outstanding hallmarks is the absence of abrasiveness or pride of personal prestige. Instead the attitude of mercy and compassion to others, accompanied by a genuine empathy, marks such people.

God places enormous emphasis upon this aspect of the Christian's behavior. Not only does He desire to see it expressed in the conduct of His followers, but, even more than that, *He insists on it.*

A study of the Scriptures soon makes this apparent.

For example in Micah 6:8 we read emphatically

> He hath shewed thee, O man,
> what is good; and what doth
> the Lord require of thee,
> but to do justly, and to love mercy,
> and to walk humbly with thy God?

Genuine, godly mercy is a quality of character not well understood by most of us—the reason being that it is essentially an attribute of God, rather than of man.

Mercy is to care, and care very deeply about one another. It is to care to the point where we are prepared to be involved with the sufferings and adversities of others. It implies that I am prepared to put myself in the other person's place. It means that I shall try to really understand why they behave as they do, even though it injures me. It is a "willingness to walk a mile in the other man's moccasins before I criticize his conduct." It is the extension of good will, help, forgiveness, compassion and kindness to one who may not seem to deserve it.

To a greater or lesser degree, all of us human beings seem well able to exhibit a fair amount of kindness. We can love those who love us. We can help those who help us. We can entertain good will toward those who are gracious to us. We can even be very kind to plants, animals, birds, pets of all kinds.

But mercy is more than this. It is much more than merely "the milk of human kindness" that flows freely through the fabric of the human family. Mercy is the strong stuff that shows kindness to those who would kill us if they could. It is compassion extended to those who would crucify us with criticism and scorn. It is caring for those who berate and belittle us without cause.

Long before I ever took God seriously or began to follow Christ in great earnestness, I was deeply distressed by the apparent abrasiveness of so many Christians. In fact, but for the patient perseverance of God's own merciful Spirit in pursuing me down the tangled trails of my own choosing, I would no doubt have ditched Christianity completely.

The one behavior pattern that repelled me again and again in God's people was their unmerciful conduct toward others. I found many of them to be kind only so long as it served their own selfish, self-centered ends. But when it came to really caring for another who might be different from them or opposed to them there was seldom any mercy shown.

In part this explains why the church, as such, has made less of an impact on society than it might have done. Far too often, Christians take a curious stance of supposed self-righteousness. They insist somehow that others are all wrong and they are all right. This finds expression in denominational differences. It erupts in harsh criticism of those whose life styles differ from theirs. It manifests itself in harsh, hard attitudes that demand much of others, even though they may be innocently in error.

The result is that, far too often, the non-Christian feels that he or she is being treated in a demeaning and patronizing manner. Even the most untutored primitive person has sufficient personal esteem and individual dignity to resent such contemptuous condescension from a so-called Christian.

True mercy is not tainted with this self-righteous attitude. Nor, on the other hand, is mercy a milk-toast tolerance for wrong in another. It is not a wishy-washy attitude of weak-kneed subservience to sin and evil in society. It is a caring concern that attempts to right wrongs without regard for the personal cost involved.

Jesus told His tough young companions that if they were in fact full of mercy, they were fortunate indeed, for in turn they would find mercy. We get what we give in life. We reap what we plant. We sow mercy and we harvest the same.

This is absolutely true. The trouble is it does not always work out in a straightforward "tit-for-tat" equation as most people feel it should. In truth it is quite a complex problem that baffles many. So let me explain a profound principle here that may help others to understand this human dilemma.

We have an old English expression—"That is a dog that bites the hand which feeds it." It implies that often in life those to whom mercy is extended turn around and injure their benefactor. It shows that frequently the merciful man or woman is simply abused, mutilated and maligned by his or her beneficiary.

There is of course the classic case of the life of our Lord. He came to His generation in mercy, love, compassion and generosity. He did nothing but good. He healed the sick, helped the suffering and bestowed happiness wherever He went. Still His generation turned against him. They scorned and abused Him. Finally they crucified Him.

Yet from His lips came that incredible cry, "Father, forgive them, for they know not what they do!" O such generosity . . . such compassion . . . such understanding.

So in seriousness, we must see that even as Christ in

His perfect deportment received little or no mercy from His beneficiaries, it is less than likely that we will.

Whence, then, does the mercy come to us of which Christ speaks? Where do we obtain our mercy? From two sources. First it often comes to us with stunning surprise from those from whom we least expected to find it. And secondly it flows to us freely from our Father God.

In my own life I am acutely aware that I am a rough-hewn man. Because of my rather tough, rough up-bringing in a frontier environment, I simply do not possess the polish of the "man about town." There are characteristics in my make-up which may seem harsh and unyielding. But, despite this, my life has been deeply touched by the mercy of those who took the time to try and understand me—who cared enough to forgive so many of my faults and who in mercy made me their friend.

Often these were people to whom I had shown no special kindness. Their bestowal of mercy on me was something totally unexpected and undeserved. Because of this, it has been a double delight. More than that, it has been an enormous inspiration that lifted and challenged me to respond in a measure beyond my wildest dreams.

Mercy does just that to people. It excites and stimulates their hope. It reassures them that life can be beautiful. It convinces them that there is good reason to carry on and push for better things if others care that much.

This all implies that if someone has extended mercy to me, surely I, in turn, can and must extend mercy to others.

But, to really find the true source of inner inspiration for this sort of conduct, the Christian simply must look beyond his fellow man. He must look away to the mercy of God our Father. Nothing else in all the world will so humble us. Nothing else will so move our stony spirits to extend mercy. Nothing else will so powerfully induce us to do the proper thing in extending genuine mercy to our contemporaries.

Without apology I quote here from my book, *A Gardener Looks at the Fruits of the Spirit:* ". . . The kindness of God has drawn me to Him with bonds of love stronger than steel. The mercy of my Lord has endeared me to Him with enormous gratitude and thanksgiving. The generous compassion and intimate care of His gracious Spirit are an enriching refreshment, new every day!

"It is extremely difficult to convey on paper, in human language, the incredible kindness of my Father, God. It seems to me that whoever attempts to do this always falls far short. This is a dimension of divine generosity that transcends our human capabilities to convey to one another. It can be experienced but it cannot be explained.

"It is the kindness of God, expressed in Christ and revealed to us by His Spirit that supplies my salvation. His kindness makes provisions for my pardon from sins and selfishness at the cost of His own laid-down life. It is His kindness that forgives my faults and accepts me into His family as His dearly beloved child. His kindness enables me to stand acquitted of my wrongdoing, justified freely in His presence. God's kindness removes my guilt and I am at once with Him and others in peace. It is the kindness of God that enables Him to share Himself with me in the inner sanctuary of my spirit, soul, and body. His kindness enables me to be re-made, refashioned, re-formed gently into His likeness. His kindness gives enormous meaning and dignity to this life and endless delight in the life yet to come." *

It is the man moved by God's mercy who looks out upon our "sick" society and is moved by compassion. Too many of us are simply too tough in our treatment of our contemporaries. We are too tough on the sinner and not tough enough on his or her sins. We have our views reversed.

---

* *A Gardener Looks at the Fruit of the Spirit* (Waco: Word Books, 1978), pp. 128–129.

In dealing with the beautiful young woman caught in the act of adultery our Lord shows us how to behave in mercy. He did not condemn her. But He insisted she should not sin again. Her sins were absolutely abhorrent to Him, because they were totally destructive of her for whom He had such enormous mercy and concern.

We are too prone to make blanket denunciations of our society. We are too quick to judge others in a general off-handed way without investigating the reasons for individual behavior. If we are to be merciful we must take the time to understand why people act as they do. And often we find it is exactly as Christ said while being crucified, "they know not what they do!"

So much of our social malaise originates in appalling ignorance. Little do people realize either the reasons for their bad behavior or the awful consequences of their misconduct.

It is for this reason that we are called upon to be light in society that will dispel the darkness of such ignorance. It is what our Master meant when He asserted that we were to be the salt that would forestall and prevent total putrefaction of our culture.

Christ calls us to be merciful. He calls us to be forgiving and compassionate. This does not mean we wink at wrong and sweep sin under the carpet. Rather it demands that we care enough to bring others to the God of all mercy. And it is He who will cleanse, re-create, and renew them in His loving-kindness and tender mercy. Bless His dear name!

# 6

# *People Pure in Heart*

△

When Christ made the categorical statement to His young companions, "Blessed are the pure in heart: for they shall see God," it was a concept bound to produce problems for them. Ever since it was first uttered, this thought of "people pure in heart" has led to endless debate by scholars.

What did Jesus really have in mind when He spoke about a person of pure heart?

First of all, we simply must face the fact that the word *heart,* as it is used in the Word of God, is often seriously misunderstood. Just as the word *love* is so often abused and misused in modern language, so *heart* likewise is not properly appreciated.

For example, it is not uncommon to see preachers and teachers place their hands over their chests while speaking and say in all solemnity, "You simply must have Christ here!" referring directly to the bodily organ in the chest which pumps blood through the circulatory system.

People glibly speak of loving God with all one's "heart." By this they imply that He is loved with all of their affection. Most readers of the Bible assume that the scores of refer-

ences made to "the heart of man" have to deal with the
seat of a man's emotions.

All in all there is a general vagueness about "the heart."
In many cases there is a definite misunderstanding. At worst
there is an actual, serious distortion of truth.

"The heart" is not the center of my emotions. It is not
the source of my feelings and sentiments. It is not the central
organ of my body somehow occupied by God.

Throughout the unique revelation given to us by the Spirit
of God in the Scriptures, the "heart" refers to my *will*.

It is in the citadel of a person's will that the final and
ultimate decisions are made as to what one shall be, where
one will go, what one will do.

Any choices we may make either with our minds or our
emotions can be quickly cancelled out and readily overridden
by our wills. In the final analysis, it is a person's will that
decides his destiny.

Positive proof of this is our absolute inability to keep
either purely mental or emotional resolutions. We may make
such decisions, completely convinced that they are either
rationally sound, intellectually proper, and emotionally appropriate. But unless the will is also so set our best intentions
come to nothing. Our intellectual or emotional choices simply fade away and are lost in the mists of memory.

This explains, for instance, why it is reported that fewer
than 5 percent of those people who claim to make decisions
(either mental or emotional) to follow Christ ever carry them
out. The simple fact is that their wills, their "hearts" have
never been touched and turned around and transformed
by the indwelling life of Christ.

On the other hand, show me the individual who through
genuine repentance, remorse and restitution of wrong sets
his/her will to serve Christ, and I will show you one whose
will is pure before God.

For to have a "pure heart" is another way of saying an
individual is utterly sincere, utterly single-minded, utterly set

in will to do God's will. This was the very key to Christ's own character when He was here among us as the Man Christ Jesus.

He iterated and reiterated, "I am come to do the will of him that sent me. . . . My meat is to do my father's will. . . . Not my will be done, but thine."

There is no duplicity, no double mindedness, no deception, no double dealing in such a person.

That is why in his epistle James is so forthright in his statement, "Draw nigh to God, and he will draw nigh to you. Cleanse your hands, ye sinners; and purify your hearts, ye double-minded" (James 4:8).

The person who beyond any sort of intellectual sophistication or emotional indulgence determines in the depths of his/her will to do God's will is bound to draw near to God. And conversely it is to such an individual of sincere intentions to whom God, in Christ, by His Spirit draws near.

This question of being "near" or "far" from God has, of course, nothing to do with physical distance. It is a matter of being in accord with God's *will*. It has to do with being in agreement with Christ. It is a question of coming into intimate harmony with the Holy Spirit.

God's declarations regarding the natural state and condition of the heart of man are utterly devastating. They shatter all our proud sophistication about the inherent decency of man. They pulverize our pride and expose the appalling pollution of our perverse wills.

For example in Jeremiah 17:9 we read, "The heart is deceitful above all things, and desperately wicked: who can know it?"

Our Lord Himself declared in Mark 7:20–23:

> That which cometh out of the man,
> that defileth the man.
> For from within, out of the heart
> of men, proceed evil thoughts,

adulteries, fornications, murders,
thefts, covetousness, wickedness,
deceit, lasciviousness, an evil eye,
blasphemy, pride, foolishness:
all these evil things come from within,
and defile the man.

Statements of this sort shatter our self-composure. If we take them seriously, we will cry out from within our innermost beings as David did so long ago: "Create in me a clean [pure] heart, O God; and renew a right spirit within me" (Ps. 51:10).

There must be a cleansing, an absolution, a profound purification of our persons if we are to be people "pure in heart." This is much more than mere soft, sentimental wishful thinking. It entails a drastic housecleaning of our wills (hearts) from their old wicked ways.

People prefer not to be told this. They prefer to just have a poultice of pious pap applied to the pollution of their "hard hearts." They do not want the deep radiation of God's searching Spirit to expose and eradicate the malignancy of a will set against God. They do not want the burning surgery of God's Word to expose the lies, duplicity and dreadful deception of a wicked will. They do not want the cleansing, sterilizing impact of the laid-down life of God in Christ— the blessed "blood" of the crucified Savior—to cleanse away the contamination of a selfish, self-centered will.

But these are the means and methods used by God to restore the sin-sick heart. They are the healing touch that transforms the will of man. They are the manner in which we are re-made and re-created as new creatures in Christ Jesus (2 Cor. 5:17).

To have a new heart is to have a new will. To have a pure heart is to have a pure will determined to do God's will.

Such a person, Christ stated emphatically, would see God. Again there is confusion in many circles, for some places in the Scriptures state unequivocally that no man can see God. Elsewhere Jesus Himself stated, "He that hath seen me, hath seen the Father" (John 14:9).

What then did our Lord mean?

He implied that the person whose will came into harmony with God's will would in truth discover the living reality of the living God. This can and does happen in various ways. He does in fact "see" God very much at work in the world. He does discover His Spirit striving with men in society. Here are some of those ways:

1) He "sees" God very much at work in his own life. There will be a definite shift in the direction and thrust of his priorities. God's interests will become his interests. The former life style will lose its allure and fascination. The new standards set by Christ will become his. He will discover that he is moving strongly in sympathy with the Spirit of God. And life will acquire an acute sense of purpose.

2) He will begin "to see" Christ in others—not only in the gentle, gracious conduct of mature and loving Christians, but even in the unlovely people. He will "see" that God is among men, often in disguise. Anything that he contributes to help and heal a broken society he is doing to Christ. He will see men as Christ sees men.

3) He will "see" God in the person of Christ. Jesus the Christ is no longer just an historical character of academic interest. He is no longer a theological moralist about whom one has doctrinal disputes. He is God very God. And He is seen as the Living Lord.

4) He will "see" God in the presence and person of the gracious Holy Spirit. His living presence as the Alongside One, the Counselor, the Comrade, the Companion who leads and guides into all truth will be vital and invigorating. For the Spirit of God is given in plenitude to the person who obeys and does God's will (Acts 5:32).

5) He will "see" the reality of God in the wonder of the created universe. He will discover that the splendor of

creation in all of its magnificent forms is but a manifestation of the mind and motives of a caring, compassionate God.

6) He will "see" God in the Word spoken and written. He will find to his unbounded delight that what Jesus declared is true, "The words that I speak unto you, they are spirit, and they are life!" He will see as John wrote so forcibly: "In the beginning was the Word, and the Word was with God, and the Word was God" (John 1:1).

7) He will "see" God very much at work in response to his own prayers and praise. He will recognize that the helping hand of God his Father is very active in his affairs. He will "see" that God is in fact at work "behind the scenes" arranging the details of his days. And in this he rejoices.

Since all of these enormous benefits and delights are the blessings of the person pure in heart, it is appropriate to ask how an individual keeps pure. How does one keep in the will of God? Are there practical ways whereby my will can be constantly aligned with God's will?

Yes, there are! And for purposes of help and simplicity they will be recapitulated here very quickly.

First, it is essential that no sin, no wrong, no evil be allowed to linger long between God and myself. If it does it impairs my vision of God. It becomes the splinter in the eye of my conscience that blinds me to the will and wishes of my Father.

This sin must be dealt with at once. It must be confessed, brought into the open, and removed from my conscience by genuine repentance. Then I am able to walk with God in the clear light of His Word, being guided by His Spirit. Read 1 John 1.

Secondly, I simply must spend time alone with God, my Father, meditating and relishing His Word. It is through the Scriptures that He discloses His desires to me. Through His Word by His own Spirit He shows me how to behave and conduct my life amid a confused society.

In this way His Word cleanses me from contamination.

It purifies my thoughts and ennobles my outlook. It directs my aspirations (Eph. 5:26 / John 15:3).

Thirdly, by keeping close company with Christ, by sensing acutely His presence on the path of life I am aware of, and sensitive to, the promptings of His own Spirit. His wishes are imparted to me as I keep myself aware of His presence. "Oh God, you are here, and your wishes are my command." *Read John 14:17.*

Finally, there is the intense and vibrant hope of Christ's coming to call me "home." There is the eager anticipation of "seeing" Him face to face as He really is. There is the thrill of at last being fully conformed to His likeness. All of these produce a most powerful purifying effect on my will.

"Behold, what manner of love the Father hath bestowed upon us, that we should be called the sons of God: therefore the world knoweth us not, because it knew him not. Beloved, now are we the sons of God, and it doth not yet appear what we shall be: but we know that, when he shall appear, we shall be like him; for we shall see him as he is. And every man that hath this hope in him purifieth himself, even as he is pure" *(1 John 3:1–3).*

As a small lad, growing up in the bush country of East Africa, I had to be sent hundreds of miles away from home to attend boarding school. Sometimes at end of term, it would be possible for Dad to drive across the terrible trails and dusty roads to fetch me home.

Perched high on the hillside I could scan the wide, hot plains for the first faint signs of a plume of dust that denoted, *"Dad is coming—Dad is coming!"* With what eagerness, what excitement, what racing pulse his arrival was anticipated.

On those days this wild, mischievous boy saw to it there were no detentions, no misconduct, no misdemeanors that would keep me from the full enjoyment of his company.

My hope of his coming was the health and wholesomeness

of my whole behavior. I became a "model" boy in anticipation of my dad's arrival.

So it can be for me with God my Father. At any instant, at any moment, His sudden appearance to take me "home" can come. Such awareness is a mighty force in keeping a person pure in heart, single-minded in spirit, wholesome in will.

# 7

# *Those Who Produce Peace*

△

When Jesus told His hot-headed young comrades that it was the peace-makers who were the fortunate people in society, they could scarcely credit the statement. Somehow, with their stormy dispositions they were sure the kingdom of God on earth could only come in by conflict, war and political upheavals.

Many of Christ's followers ever since that day have held the same violent views. The history of the Church and Christendom in general has not been one of perpetual peace. There have been all sorts of heated and angry disputes. There have been cruel inquisitions. There have been endless "crusades," all in the name of Christ.

Not only have there been deep doctrinal differences within the community of Christians themselves, but also enormous divergence of views over the role of Christians within society in general. The seemingly never-ending debates and diatribes that are carried on have always pained me deeply as a person. It has grieved me no end to see the so-called "children of God" wound and injure one another in wordy warfare the world around.

Because of all this belligerence it has been wrongly assumed by some that a "peace-maker" was essentially a person who went around patching up differences. It has been thought our Lord was referring only to those individuals who tried, by their own personal charm or political influence, to bring opposing parties to the peace-table. It was frequently assumed the peace-maker was one who poured oil on the troubled waters of a war-torn world.

In part, but only in small part, is this the case. For again, as in the preceding discussions of a Christian's character, our Lord was not so much concerned with what a person did, as what his inner attitudes were.

Because so much is made of peace both in the press and in the visual media, people have come to consider it the ultimate attainment. Our present generation in particular is prepared and determined to have peace at any price. If any leader should suddenly appear on the world scene who could offer and guarantee peace, he would have the whole race of mankind at his feet.

Like the word *love*, we bandy the word *peace* about in a loose and general way without fully grasping its true significance. Peace is much more than mere quietude. It is more than mere absence of conflict. It is more than sterility or stagnation in the social scene.

Peace in its truest and most powerful form is the pervasive influence of love expressed to others in good will, harmony, contentment and good cheer.

Now this is very simple to state in words on the page of a book. It is infinitely more difficult to express in the stressful experiences of a tension-ridden society. For say what we may, the interaction of people with one another always produces problems. We live in a world of strain, stress and storms in the stream of life.

Even the most noble people and finest individuals find themselves abused and attacked by their fellows. Our Lord Himself, God very God, perfect in character, impeccable in conduct, was attacked, vilified and crucified by his contemporaries. If it happened to Him, we can fully expect the same fate to befall us.

No, we do not live lives of peace and tranquillity. Jesus Himself declared emphatically, "If the world hate you, ye know that it hated me, before it hated you!" (John 15:18).

We live in an atmosphere of antagonism, an environment of enmity. Yet amid such adversity Christ calls us to produce peace.

This peace is love quietly, strongly, persistently meeting every onslaught against it with good will. It is that inner attitude of tranquillity and tolerance in the face of angry attacks. It is the willingness to accept the assaults of others even at the price of personal humiliation. It implies that even though my enemies and detractors may be at war with me I can be at peace with them.

This principle of producing peace was of course best exemplified in the life of our Lord. For though He did nothing but good amongst men, his jealous opponents were determined to destroy Him. When they had done their very worst and he hung in burning shame and agony upon the cross, a tough Roman centurion looked upon His bruised and broken body to exclaim: "Surely, this man was the son of God!"

For though Christ had been reviled, He did not revile in return. Though He had been falsely accused, He did not react in flaming anger. Instead, He was silent before His assailants, asking only in quiet tones, "Why do you do this to me?" Of course they really did not know. Steeped in their own sin and selfishness, it was impossible for them to see the enormity of their evil. It is always thus with men at war with others. So from the depths of His Spirit, Christ cried out, "Father, forgive them, for they know not what they do!"

We must do the same.

There can be no other path to peace.

We simply do not sit on our little pedestals of pride and self-importance hurling imprecations at others who attack us. Rather we bow humbly and beseech our Father to keep us from sinning in the pride of self-righteous justification.

Perhaps no person ever better demonstrated this in his everyday life than my dad. As a lay person he felt God's special call to give his life in humble service to Africa.

In no sense could he ever be considered a scholar, theologian, academic or sophisticated professional in the ranks of Christian workers. Yet in a unique and unusual manner, God's hand of blessing rested upon his endeavors. He established hundreds of churches, and in his short life saw thousands of Africans come to Christ.

Because of this he became the object of vicious and cruel attacks from others. He was regarded with envious jealousy and contempt by those who saw his work flourish. He was accused falsely even by his so-called friends.

Yet again and again he said to me as a growing lad, "Son, 'when a man's ways please the Lord, he maketh even his enemies to be at peace with him' " (Prov. 16:7). This was literally true in his life. For when he suddenly died at the early age of 54, many of his fiercest antagonists attended his funeral out of deep honor and genuine respect for a truly good and great man.

In fact, many were forced to declare, "This man was a son of God." "He was a producer of peace." He had lived and labored among them only in good will even under attack.

So we must, if we are Christ's followers, ask ourselves the sobering, searching questions, "Am I a producer of peace in society? Do I generate good cheer and godliness?"

If this is not so, if instead my life is a constant battle ground of belligerence and ill will, it is essential to take a hard look at my character. Am I really God's person in my society? Am I able to be a light in a world of wretched warfare? Am I able to be salt for all the terrible tension of my times? Am I contributing anything of contentment and consolation to my contemporaries? Am I a peace-maker? Or do I just produce problems and pain for those around me?

How does one live in peace amid such a stressful society? Here are a few simple suggestions.

1) It is understood here that peace-makers are people who have already discovered what it means to be poor in spirit. They have known what it is to come under the control of Christ. They have seen God very much at work in their daily experience. They are subject to the supreme Sovereignty of God's gracious Spirit.

Such people will be prepared to cry out, "O God, invade the whole of our beings with Your presence. Shed abroad, within our souls (mind, emotions, will) all of Your love that will find full expression in attitudes and actions of peace."

If expressed in utter sincerity and total honesty, God will take such requests seriously. He will respond in making Himself available to the seekers. And though all the circumstances of life seem charged with hostility and animosity, they will be able to live at peace with others who may wish to be at war with them. They will be recognized uniquely as children of God.

2) Amid the stress and strain of society God's Spirit will enable us to control our minds and emotions and wills. The harsh word will not be spoken. The cutting sarcasm will not be indulged. The destructive choices will not be made. Those attitudes and activities that we ordinarily employ to justify our actions and achieve our own selfish ends will be set aside.

We do not just think about this sort of thing in idle wishful thinking. Instead we determine to do God's will in our situation. We recognize and acknowledge, "O God, it is You who must work in me both to will and do Your good and peaceable pleasure."

3) In any given experience, no matter how explosive it may seem, no matter how freighted with friction, no matter

how unfair or unjust it appears, we can ask our constant
Companion, "O Christ, what would You do?"

After all He is here! We are in this stressful situation
together! I am not bearing the abuse alone!

God is in it with me. Together we must endure the brunt
of the attacks. Together we will walk through it in quiet
strength and noble serenity as His Spirit guides us.

4) Let us learn to be generous, gracious, great-hearted
people in our attitudes toward those who oppose us. This
requires the grace of God. The grace of God is nothing
less than the very life of God given to me in rich supply
by His presence with me.

It is the capacity to put myself in the other person's position. It is the ability to try and identify with him/her in their
dilemma. It is the willingness to try and understand what
another's point of view is.

If necessary it may mean being ready to apologize. It
may mean taking a lowly position. It may mean being ready
to extend forgiveness and compassion.

Peace does not just fall into our laps like an overripe
plum that tumbles from a tree. It takes time and trouble
and thought to pursue and produce it. It comes only by
careful cultivation.

5) In our relationships with others, if we are to be at
peace, there must be a certain element of natural, honest,
open behavior on our part. We simply cannot afford to be
phony or pretentious.

If we live without a false front, others will know where
they stand with us. Though in some cases there may be
definite personality clashes, we will never be accused of duplicity or deception. Even the worst of our detractors will
come to appreciate our sincerity and integrity.

It is absurd even to expect that everyone can agree with
us. As God's people, we are bound to have deep convictions.
It is proper to hold to these with enormous tenacity.

Still this does not mean that we need to become abusive

and belligerent toward those who oppose us or differ with us. We can conduct ourselves with quiet dignity and charitable decency.

In this we will be carrying out our Father's wish for us to live in peace with all men, in so far as that is possible.

A touch of humor, a bit of light-hearted good-will, an element of cheer and wholesome laughter will often defuse the most dangerous confrontations.

6) Be prepared to be deflated. Be willing to take the lowly place. Be ready to humble yourself, not only beneath the hand of God, but also beneath the much more abrasive hand of man.

Realize in all honesty that if you desire to be conformed to the character of Christ, then it will require the shaping and polishing of your life by the cutting, scraping, sandpapering rub of rough people and rough circumstances.

This is our Father's way of turning out truly fine characters. They are not only shaped in the stillness of our solitude, but also on the millstones of stress and strain within the society of men. As your pride goes, peace comes.

7) Give thanks for not only the good things and gentle people in your life, but also for the hard circumstances and difficult individuals.

Remind yourself that all of these, if indeed you are God's child, have actually been arranged by your Father with your best interests in mind. Accept them as His special plan for your ultimate benefit. Approve of them as His provision for accomplishing His very optimistic purposes in your total, external experience with Him.

As you do this deliberately, honestly, earnestly, the peace of God which passes all understanding will flood your whole being. It will pour out of you to touch and heal those around you. You will be a peace-maker, a child of God!

# 8

# *Persecuted People*

△

The last special quality of character mentioned by our Lord was that of suffering. He knew with unerring assurance that anyone who forsook all to follow Him would be persecuted. The person whose life and character would make an impact on society was bound to be abused.

On first thought this may have seemed to be an absurd statement to His companions. After all, was it not the person of high principles, of lofty ideals, of fine behavior who drew applause and recognition from his fellows? Does society not heap its honors upon the individual who serves its causes and contributes to its welfare? Is it not true that accolades come to the people who perform well?

In part this is true. There have been the Dr. Doolittles, the Mother Teresas, the Albert Schweitzers. But there have also been the Martin Luther Kings, the Joan of Arcs, the Abraham Lincolns who paid dearly with their very lives.

For many years as a struggling young Christian I was led to believe that if I was just good enough, and kind enough, and loving enough, the whole of the world would be bound to hug me to its heart. Unfortunately and unhappily one learns in time that simply is not so. It is one of the sobering shocks that comes to us as mature Christians.

If God, very God, who was all perfection, suffered such abuse at the hands of His adversaries when He was here among us as the Man Christ Jesus, how can we expect less? What leads us to think we will be exempt from suffering? What absurdity it is to assume that we can escape the persecution He endured if we are His people!

Just before His death, Jesus discussed this whole matter in great detail with His disciples. He was determined that they should not be left in the dark about it. He did not want them deluded.

> If the world hate you,
> ye know that it hated me before it
> hated you.
>
> If ye were of the world,
> the world would love his own:
> but because ye are not of the world,
> but I have chosen you out of the world,
> therefore the world hateth you.
>
> Remember the word that I said unto you,
> The servant is not greater than his lord.
> If they have persecuted me,
> they will also persecute you;
> if they have kept my saying,
> they will keep yours also.
>
> But all these things will they do
> unto you for my name's sake,
> because they know not him that sent me.
> (John 15:18–21).

It is essential for us to understand clearly what Christ really meant by His comments. There is much confusion in Christian circles about suffering and persecution. It is also worthy of special note that of all the eight attributes of Christian character, this is the only one our Lord dealt with in depth, twice over. Therefore it does demand our special study.

First it must be understood emphatically that the persecution would come not because we were odd, queer, or absurd in our conduct. It would come because we are righteous. Secondly we would not be singled out for abuse because we were bellicose or belligerent, but for Christ's sake.

It needs to be stated here that Christians are not called to be exhibitionists. Nowhere in God's Word are we exhorted to indulge in theatrics and grandiose displays of super-spirituality. God, by His Spirit, does not instruct us to create a carnivallike atmosphere in which to do His work in the world.

Some Christians draw public attention to themselves by outlandish conduct. They incite the interest of the media by bizarre behavior. They attract abuse by absurd life styles or outrageous and arrogant public statements. They really deserve no better.

But Christ does not call us to that sort of thing. Anyone who has read this far will realize that God insists His people be gracious in spirit, humbled in heart, easily entreated, disciplined to do His work in the world with mercy, peace and good will.

This being the case, it is perfectly proper and legitimate to ask, why then are such people so often persecuted? Why are those who live righteous lives so often wronged? Why all through human history has *Cain* attacked *Abel?*

The answer to this eternal enigma is embedded in several profound principles. Once we understand them we will find it much less difficult to endure suffering for Christ's sake.

1) Good and evil are mutually exclusive. Truth and deception are always opposed. Decency and degradation abhor each other. Righteousness and wrong-doing are *ever* at war.

In the very nature of things this is so. It is the only valid explanation for the suffering, pain and pathos that form the fabric of human history. This is God our Father's unique disclosure to us.

2) The evil person, the wrong-doer, the decadent individual, no matter who he/she may be, always feels threatened by the righteous. They feel their own position is imperiled by the person who behaves righteously. They feel a certain unease and even outrage in the face of righteous behavior.

So the natural, instinctive reaction is to try to eliminate the threat by outright attack, abuse or condemnation.

3) The great majority of society simply is not moral. To claim so is an absurdity. All through the Scriptures it is made abundantly clear that "the righteous" are always a minority. God's people are always a peculiar little remnant. Christ's church is always a small handful. His followers are ever a little flock.

We are noncomformists. We don't fit comfortably into the man-made mould of our contemporaries. So we are selected as suitable targets for attack.

This abuse will come whether we deserve it or not. The cunning craftiness of our adversaries will leave no stone unturned to bury us with belligerence. The noble *Joseph* was dragged down into a dark dungeon. The righteous *Elijah* was threatened with cold-blooded murder. The impeccable *Daniel* was dumped into a lion's den. That saint of God, Watchman Nee, languished in a Chinese prison for twenty-three years. Thousands of Kenyan Christians were tortured and burned to death during the years of the Mau-Mau terrorism.

All down the long centuries during which God has called out certain people to be His own, they have suffered and endured appalling persecution. Not all of them were rescued and saved from their distress. Not all of them were restored to places of prestige and prominence like *Joseph, Elijah,* and *Daniel.* There have been those who perished, and died terrible deaths like Peter, Paul, Watchman Nee and ten thousand upon ten thousand other righteous martyrs.

Please read Hebrews 11:32–40 carefully.

The anguish, the sorrow, the privation, the sadness, the

pain, the suffering of Christ's own all down the ages stands as stark, irrefutable evidence of what our Lord said. Those who in the contemporary church of our Western world, claim that Christians need not suffer are speaking out of the depths of enormous ignorance.

Any man, any woman, who will determine to live righteously for Christ's sake will suffer persecution (2 Tim. 3:12). And in passing it must be said here that the attacks made upon him may not always necessarily come just from the unrighteous.

Sad to say some of the grievous and painful persecution may come from his own so-called brethren. Often these are carnal Christians, worldlings, made uncomfortable by the commitment of their more devout "friends." It will be the fellow believers who often almost devour each other (Gal. 5:15).

In the face of all this conflict, how then does Christ's follower go on to live a godly, quiet and joyous life despite his detractors? How do we discover that in truth it is "blessed" to suffer for Christ's sake? How does one find the great reward in heaven for all the heartache?

There are three rather straightforward, simple answers to these questions.

1) If in truth persecution does come to me because of my righteous character and commendable, Christlike conduct, it is proof positive that I am indeed God's person. This becomes a quiet, serene, inner assurance to my spirit that I am in truth His son.

It was our Lord Himself who declared without hesitation, "Woe unto you, when all men shall speak well of you! For so did their fathers to the false prophets" (Luke 6:26).

An infallible test of our testimony for God lies in whether or not it tickles everyone's ears. If we are popular people in whom the world can see no wrong, it is high time to assess where we stand in a society set against God.

It is the person somewhat shunned by his companions,

somewhat ostracized by his associates, held at arm's length by his contemporaries, persecuted for his love of God, who can inwardly rejoice over his identity as a child of God.

Because he speaks truth, lives truth, reveals truth it polarizes other people just as Christ did. Some will become his beloved friends and brothers in the family of God. Others will endeavor to bury him six feet under the ground with their belligerence. They will try to silence him.

2) The second remarkable realization that comes to the Christian under attack is the acute awareness that this world, this society, this earth scene of which he is a part really is not his permanent residence. This is not an enduring domicile. He will not be here for long. He is simply a pilgrim passing through.

All of this has been stated hundreds of times before by scholars, saints and those who seek "a better and more enduring dimension of life." What astonishes me is how very few of us live as "transients."

We simply do not have "eternity burned upon our eyeballs." We are mesmerized by the materialism of our modern culture. We are preoccupied with our possessions, our position in society, our prestige. We act as though this show will go on forever. We live as if the stage curtains will never fall on our brief little earth scene.

But here and there a scattering of God's people really are aware they are merely travelers passing through. They see themselves as citizens of another "country," residents of another realm, transients en route "home." It is not surprising, then, that we should feel ill-at-ease here. We really don't fit that well into the culture of our contemporaries. We are uncomfortable in the society estranged from our God and our Father.

In all of this there is reassurance to us. We know with intense awareness "O Father, I am going home!" It is this anticipation, this joy, this hope which sustained Christ all through the cruel abuse He suffered while here. In similar fashion it can be our source of enormous strength in our struggles here.

This does not mean that our Father does not grant us quiet resting places, shady oases and still waters along the route. He does, in generous measure! But the trail we tramp with Him through a hostile world will also be tough, steep and sometimes dreadfully dangerous before we reach higher ground.

3) The third wondrous reward that can attend persecution for God's people is the actual foretaste and preview it provides of heaven on earth . . . now.

Jesus said simply, "Rejoice and be exceeding glad for great is your reward in heaven!" Too many of us, for far too long, have been taught that there is only "pie in the sky." We have been led to believe erroneously that heaven was some remote habitation in outer space awaiting our future arrival.

Heaven begins here when we become God's child. It is a dimension of delightful living with Christ about which our worldly associates know nothing. It is righteousness and peace and joy in company with God's gracious Spirit which is totally foreign to the non-Christian (Rom. 14:17).

Let me illustrate:

Recently I came under vicious attack from some of my colleagues. For reasons still unknown to me all sorts of false accusations were hurled at me. There was a fierce outpouring of abuse, venom and vituperation. It went on and on and on.

How does one react? How does one respond? How does one rejoice?

For days and days I was silent. I sought God's special guidance. I wrote and rewrote letters of reply. Finally God's gentle Spirit enabled me to act and live and behave exactly as our Lord did, "Who, when he was reviled, reviled not again; when he suffered, he threatened not; but committed himself to him that judgeth righteously!" (1 Pet. 2:23).

So that hour, that night, righteousness from God flowed into my spirit. Peace from the Prince of Peace permeated my soul. Joy, given in generous overflowing measure, was given to me by the Comforter, my Companion, the Spirit of God.

Then heaven came down and glory (the very character of Christ) filled my soul. So I slept in serenity as a child of God.

Yes, in truth, in fact, in reality our reward can be in heaven, now!

# Part III

---

*Salt for Society*

# *INTRODUCTION*

△

Having completed His summation of what a Christian's character should be, the Master made a most remarkable statement. He turned to look on His eager young companions, so full of enthusiasm and youthful vigor, and remarked in quiet simplicity, *"You are the salt of the earth."*

To us in the sophisticated society of our late twentieth century this statement, on the surface, might seem of minor significance. But to Jesus' companions it bore profound personal meaning.

For most of us in the Western world salt is a very common condiment used in cooking. We generally have a shaker of it set on our tables with which to spice up our food. We also use it in enormous quantities on our highways in winter to help melt the ice and snow—which of course also accelerates the rate at which our automobiles rust out. And lastly, for those who live near the sea, the presence of salt in ocean water and ocean air is a prominent part of life.

But in our Lord's day, salt was, without a doubt, the most important element in the culture of His contemporaries.

Salt was so special, so unique, so sought after in some societies that it was actually regarded as more valuable than gold. It was used in some countries as the medium of exchange, the basis of barter.

There were in ancient times famous "salt routes" which traversed all of the Middle East. Caravans of camels, donkeys and mules transported tons of salt across hundreds of miles of torturous terrain. These notorious "salt routes" criscrossed Northern Africa, the whole of the Mediterannean Basin, the entire Middle East and extended even as far as the subcontinent of India. Both men and beasts were considered utterly expendable in the ruthless, competitive salt trade.

People of primitive societies were virtual connoisseurs of salt. It was much more than a common ingredient of their everyday diet. For many it was a valuable and rare delicacy. Because much of it was gathered from natural "salt pans," great desert wastes, or distant ocean edges, it varied significantly in quality, taste and pungency.

Enormous prices would be paid for "pure" salt, not contaminated by other mineral elements. Salt of intense pungency was so highly esteemed that men thought nothing of risking their very lives to obtain it.

Even in places as remote as the Hawaiian Islands, the early, primitive people would launch daring sea voyages in their canoes to reach the south Puna Coast of the Big Island of Hawaii, for the salt collected there was considered the finest anywhere in the island chain. Often these excursions to obtain the best salt were charged with enormous risk as the Hawaiians crossed the open ocean between islands to obtain their favorite condiment.

Even as a young man, growing up among the primitive tribespeople of East Africa, I was always deeply impressed by the insatiable appetite of Africans for salt. It was something they sought with single-minded determination. They would have it at any cost. To obtain it they would trek great distances through the bush, across the plains and over the hills. Salt was an absolute necessity for survival. It was utterly essential to life itself. Why?

In Christ's society, and in the context of the culture in which He lived, salt had at least seven main functions peculiar to His people. The next seven chapters will be based on these functions—salt for maintaining health, preserving, seasoning, healing, meeting livestock needs, symbolizing loyalty and friendship and offering of sacrifice.

# 9

# *Health for Society*

△

Salt is the very key to health, strength and the vigor of people who live in hot climates. It is an essential ingredient for proper body metabolism. The normal exchange and retention of fluids within the cells depends upon the salt present.

Where heat is intense or humidity is high, the body becomes subject to enormous stress through the loss of moisture and salt in perspiration. The body is desiccated. It loses its strength. Life processes become impaired. Weakness sets in. And death may occur unless salt and water are replenished.

This explains why miners who work down in the depths of hot mine shafts and engineers who work in the awful heat of great boiler rooms of ships or factories are issued an extra ration of salt tablets every day. They simply must have this ingredient in their diet if they are to perform their duties satisfactorily.

So it was among the common people of Jesus' time. They did not have the benefit of modern buildings or special air conditioning to protect them from the fierce heat of their semidesert climate. Exposed to intense sunlight and high temperatures most of the year, the Palestinian people simply had to have salt to survive. It was essential for their very health and well-being. It was a key to strength and vitality in a rough climate and tough terrain.

Looking at His young, eager companions Jesus said: "You are to be that same element in society. You are to be that ingredient amongst men which will contribute to their health, their vigor, their very well being."

It is worthy of our special attention to realize and always remember that whatever salt is applied to, it invariably penetrates. It does not lie inert upon the surface.

Second only to its peculiar pungency, the other unique quality of this remarkable condiment is its power to penetrate. Put a mere pinch of it in a jug of water and all of the water becomes salty. Take a tiny taste of it on the tip of your tongue and in a few minutes it will have permeated the whole of your body.

Our Lord was saying to His followers, and He says the same to us today: "You, my followers, are the salt which simply must permeate and penetrate society if it is to have health and stability."

There is an unfortunate tendency among some Christians to withdraw from society. There lurks the inclination to retreat into sheltered and secluded situations where we are anything but salt to our contemporaries.

At no time, nor in any instance, did Jesus, the Christ, instruct His disciples to remain aloof and apart from the common people. He did not set up secluded societies or sheltered enclaves in which His followers were to be excluded from the stresses and strains of human society.

Rather we find Him making concerted efforts to actually send His men into the mainstream of the world in which they lived. "I send you out as sheep amongst wolves." "I send you out to the lost sheep of the house of Israel." "As the Father has sent me into the world, so send I you into the world."

He was in actual fact injecting salt into society. He wanted the character, conduct and compassion of His comrades to penetrate every part of the little world in which He and they lived. Though they were to be different; though they were to bear a peculiar potency; though they were to be prominent in their powerful pungency still they were to penetrate their world.

He said to them in simple, uncomplicated, pungent language—"Go . . . preach . . . heal the sick, cleanse the lepers, raise the dead, cast out devils: freely you have received, freely give!" (Matt. 10:6-8).

He asked no more of them than He did of Himself. It was this same Jesus, God very God, who was scorned as the friend of publicans and sinners. It was He who went about doing good. It was He who brought good tidings, who bound up the broken-hearted, who liberated the captives, who comforted those who mourned, who gave beauty for ashes, who injected strength and integrity into the society of which He was a part.

And He calls us to the same service.

He sends us into similar situations.

He intends that we contribute to the strength and health and well-being of our little world.

May I repeat here that this cannot be done by remaining aloof, remote and detached from the society of one's contemporaries.

To penetrate, salt must be applied.

To permeate, it must be present.

To perform, it must impregnate.

The uniqueness of Christianity in the community of man is the willingness of its members to be lost in the giving of themselves for the common good. We must be prepared to lose our lives, laying them down in self-giving for the sake of others.

Salt loses itself, loses its special identity, loses its unique "separateness" as it penetrates and performs its functions. Yet the powerful paradox is that these functions are only achieved by virtue of the salt's own inherent potency.

This is a difficult concept for Christians to grasp. We are in the world of men. Yet we are not of the world. We have as the source of our potency and power the unique and special pungency of the presence of God in Christ by His Spirit.

Salt is a remarkable and unusual combination of two chemical elements, sodium (Na), and chlorine (Cl). United as one (NaCl), they form a formidable compound—one essential to life.

Similarly our lives combined with Christ's life—our humanity combined with His divinity, our spirits combined with His Spirit—become the great force for good in society.

Our work in the world, our words spoken and uttered in society, our way of life are not just ours, but God and ours combined. Jesus iterated and reiterated this over and over. He said: "The words which I speak; the work which I do; the will which I carry out are not just mine, but also the Father's."

We as Christ's followers must see, and see very clearly, that we are not in society working *for* God. Nor are we in society just working *for* men. It is not a matter of us functioning somehow in our own fallible way, apart from God and apart from men. Quite the contrary, we are actively and energetically at work in the world *with* God, and *with* men.

This concept is not merely a play on words. It is not just a matter of exchanging one preposition for another. It is a profound principle which can alter and energize the whole of our life experience.

It explains why our Lord emphasized over and over that He was *with* us. He insisted that He and the Father were *One*. He promised repeatedly that He would not leave us on our own, that His presence by His Spirit would be in us, with us, always.

No matter what our calling may be in life, no matter what career God may have put us into, no matter what contribution we may be able to make to our generation, it is not something done alone.

God and I are in this together. We are doing it in society as a joint endeavor. We are giving strength, stamina, vigor and well-being as we work, live, and cooperate with one another—Christ in me, me in Him.

This is what it means to be a Christian in the contemporary world scene of any society, any culture, anywhere.

The impact made by me or any other Christian is not by virtue of my personal peculiarity, but by virtue of the living presence and vital person of the living Lord active in my body, soul, spirit.

The sum total of the contribution made upon my contemporaries is directly proportional to the degree to which I no longer see my "self" as the salt in society, but I see the very life of the living God acting as the agency in me that strengthens society.

It is His strength. It is His Spirit. It is His wisdom. It is His compassion. It is His integrity. It is His justice. It is His love. It is His faithfulness. It is His righteousness. It is His peace. It is His attributes, His fruits and His characteristics which find their expression in my character and so make their impact on the world in which I live. It should be said of me as it was of Christ, *"He is the visible expression of the invisible God!"*

A better world can only come about by better men.

A saner, stronger society can only be built by more sanctified individuals.

A stable culture can only be created by the energetic contribution of men in whom Christ is the conditioner of their characters.

If we are to be salt which penetrates society imparting

stamina, serentiy and solidity to it, we ourselves must be of that caliber. We influence others for God only to the extent in which He influences us by His own indwelling presence.

In the arts, in science, in commerce, in industry, in politics, in any area of human endeavor, we can be salt, *with God* working in us, both to will and to do His own good pleasure. We are the potent salt which He expects us to be. We can be a source of health for our society.

# 10

# *A Preservative for Society*

△

When our Lord looked fondly at His little band of would-be followers and said plainly, *"You are the salt of the earth,"* they immediately knew what He meant. They were to be a preserving element in society just as salt was the common preservative used in their daily diet.

We of the modern Western world have no clear idea of the essential role of salt in primitive societies. We take for granted the use of such processes as refrigeration, canning, packaging and chemical additives for the preservation of food from putrefaction. But such sophisticated scientific methods simply were not available in Jesus' time, nor are they in many primitive societies even today.

As a youngster growing up in the frontier environment of East Africa I lived a spartan life without all the comforts and niceties of twentieth century technology. Even though we lived at the equator under severe tropical conditions we never had a refrigerator in our home until I was eighteen years old. We simply did not resort to such complex methods of preserving meat, fish, fruit or vegetables as canning or bottling.

My parents, as well as the people around us, relied on the simple use of salt to save any extra flesh or food that could not be consumed at once. If a beef animal was butchered or a sheep slaughtered, all the meat not used immediately was always salted down for future use.

This was absolutely imperative. Under the high temperatures and hot weather of the region, decay and decomposition of meat was astonishingly rapid. We had no winter weather or cool, frosty nights to chill the flesh.

Besides this, swarms of ubiquitous flies soon hovered over the butchered carcasses. The only way to prevent them from ruining the meat with their crawling hordes of maggots was to soak the slabs of meat in a strong solution of salt.

Tons and tons of beef, lamb, and wild game meat were cut up into slender strips of flesh that were soaked in salt solution. These would then be hung to dry in the fierce sunlight, thus becoming what we called "Bill-Tong" or as it is known in North America, "Jerky." All I ever took with me when I went hunting was a few slabs of this salted meat in my back pocket. It was a nourishing trek food. It was Spartan fare, but tremendously strengthening.

What was true of meat applied to fish, fruit and other foods which people wished to preserve. We lived only seven miles from the water, high in the hills, overlooking the shores of Lake Victoria. There the African fishermen caught huge quantities of Tilapia, their favorite food fish. Because they could not possibly consume all they caught in their nets, the surplus were always split open, salted, then dried in the sun. These were then taken to market and bartered for other food.

The overpowering odor of these dried fish, being carried across the country on the heads of those who transported them in the heat, was an unforgettable smell. One could easily detect the stench on the air. And, but for the preserving presence of salt, the whole mass would have decomposed into a repulsive, rotting heap of putrefaction.

So everywhere, at all times, large quantities of salt were

being used by the common people to preserve what food they could find. It was the basic ingredient used in prolific abundance to forestall spoilage and stave off starvation and hunger. Salt was essential to survival.

In so many words, not spoken, yet implied, Jesus was saying: *"You as my followers are to play the same role in society. You are to be the element which preserves it from complete corruption. You are to preserve it from total decay."*

It is essential for men of every generation to be reminded that no matter how sophisticated a society may appear to be, there lies within its communal body the so-called "seeds" of its own demise. There is inherent in any social organization devised by man's ingenuity the inevitable elements of eventual break-down and dissolution.

The tragic story of human history bears constant witness to the inherent weaknesses of human nature and human behavior. It matters not what civilization has arisen to spread its influence upon the earth, always there is an inevitable decline from the pinnacle of purity and power to the point of ultimate declension and deterioration.

Regardless of how grand, glorious and even godly the foundations of a society may have been, eventually that society falters and fails from adverse forces at work within its own form. The basic cause for this failure is simply the inherent waywardness and selfishness of human beings.

Man, in his more noble and lofty moments, may very well be altruistic, generous and even compassionate toward his contemporaries. Yet ultimately even the best of intentions are subverted. Then people, because of their selfish, self-centered, sinful condition succumb to the lure of affluence, ease, pleasure, and power.

Only the restraining influence of the presence of God in a person's life can counteract this downward drift. Only the total transformation of human character can slow the sure slide into subversive and destructive life styles.

Only the quickening, preserving power of God's Spirit

in a soul can save it from succumbing to corruption by its contemporaries.

It is becoming fashionable to scorn the idea of sin in society. The impact of humanistic thinking is to belittle the concept that man is corrupt. Psychologists and psychiatrists would persuade us that people really are not responsible for their wrongs. Rather, the view of sociologists is that the environment is all wrong.

Their cry is, "Change society and you will get better men and women!" It simply does not happen.

Christ's call is, "Change men and women and you will get a better society! " This does work. It always has.

So the Master's thrust is that those who would follow Him are to be the salt that preserves society's usefulness, that preserves its lofty ideals, that preserves its highest standards.

It is not easy to do this. It is not easy to move and live counter to the current of corruption that flows so strongly in society. It is not easy to be different from those who drift with the crowd, who take the line of least resistance. It is not easy to take a tough stand against evil and injustice and exploitation. It is not easy to be scrupulously honest in business, industry, education or politics when others are not.

But someone has to do this if society is to be saved from savagery and social mayhem. Someone has to be bold enough to be branded a reactionary. Someone has to have enough strength to stand against the tide of perversion that floods the world. Someone has to say fearlessly, "This is right—that is wrong." "This is uplifting and constructive— that is demoralizing and destructive! "

We as God's people may be falsely accused by our contemporaries for our convictions and our conduct. We may be labeled "pious prudes." We may be taunted for truth. We may be harassed for "wearing halos." We may be maligned for following the Master.

Yet amidst all this He calls us to be the salt that saves

our society. Not because we are "great guys," but because He is a "Great God."

It may well be asked, "How is this done in a practical way? How do I as an individual contribute to the preservation of the finest qualities in my society and culture?"

First and foremost as God's people we need to become utterly fearless in our defense of God's Word. Without apology we must accept it as a unique, inspired, divine revelation as to our Father's wishes and will for us. But beyond this we must also see it as our very clear standard of behavior and personal conduct.

We must recognize that there is no other final reference point for the conduct of society and human relationships. Unhappily not only lay people, but many preachers in our pulpits are prepared to compromise the commands of Christ with human conduct. Many advocate coming to terms with the downward drift of our times.

This simply is not acceptable. We as Christians have a royal responsibility to stand surely and securely upon the Scriptures. We have a mandate from the Most High God to proclaim His desires and decrees to a decadent society.

Without hesitation we should be bold enough to openly advocate high morals, decency and integrity in human affairs. There are some carnal Christians who might prefer to come to some easy accommodation with their contemporaries. But we are not called to compromise, we are instructed to be salt. Salt has a pungency, a potency and a penetrating power that makes it a preservative, repugnant to the forces of evil and decomposition.

This may well mean that we shall not be popular nor acclaimed in the press. But by the same measure it will mark us out as people of positive and purifying influence in the affairs of our world.

Each of us can be a potent, uplifting force for good and for God in any area of the country in which we live, any segment of society in which we serve.

Second, our life style, our personal conduct, our character should be such that we deter and deflect the decadence all around us. It is utterly stupendous how one man with God can actually be a majority . . . provided his motives and personal behavior are simple, sincere and without guile.

There simply is no greater impact one can make upon family, friends or associates than that of transparent honesty, utter sincerity and wholesome integrity. It is the people with those characteristics who are "believed." They are the ones whose deportment acts as a remarkable deterrent to wrong all around them in every guise.

Third, it is essential that we be saturated with the Scriptures. The Word of God must be to us much, much more than merely *The Bible,* a book studied and read as a ritual. Rather, the words which our Lord speaks, transmitted to us by His gracious Spirit, must become spirit and life to us. It is the impress of this Word, the thrust of God's Spirit, which will preserve both us and those around us from perishing.

Fourth, it must be understood that as Christians we do not stand apart from our society. We are not aloof to the woes of our world. We do not disengage ourselves from the inexorable decay all around us.

As pungent people, empowered by the presence of Christ's Spirit within our spirits, we actually penetrate problem areas. We do become involved. We are ready to lay our lives on the line to lift those sinking in sin around us. This is not to meddle in other people's affairs, but rather to lift them from degradation.

It matters not what our vocation or avocation in life may be. Every area of human activity, every field of human enterprise can feel the impact of our presence there. We do not come to condemn, censure and criticize. We come to lift, energize, and bring an element of new life. We bear tidings of great joy. We bring an awareness of the goodness of our God.

Fifth, in all of this we need to be positive people. Too

many Christians are negative. There is a demand for us to offer others a better and more noble alternative to the degenerate life styles. We should be known and noted for our positive, dynamic approach to all of life.

Let us build better houses; let us manufacture more reliable products; let us deliver more courteous service; let us be punctual, polite people; let us produce finer music; let us write better books, plays and film scripts; let us share generously of our wealth; let us be strong for what is right and terribly tough on what is wrong; let us do something beautiful for our Father; let us keep fit, healthy and alert; let us live in great dignity and decency; let us fight for freedom, justice and equality of opportunity; let us produce better crops, livestock and food of a hundred sorts to feed a starving world; let us preserve natural beauty and all other God-given resources.

In ten thousand ways, in ten thousand places, God's people can be salt in society. We are not here to sit idly wringing our hands in despair—we are here to put our bodies, minds, emotions, wills and spirit to work with God for His benefit to those about us.

We may be in the minority amid a world roaring down the road to self-destruction. But here and there amidst the mob, we can flash the warning signs of impending disaster. Here and there, we can show others an alternate route apart from the main highway of human mayhem. Here and there, some will see the perils of their pursuits. Some will turn to follow the paths of righteousness. Here and there, some will turn to meet the Master.

And in all of this some will be saved. Among our generation, we will be salt to preserve society from perishing. And when we are gone, it will be said of us in sincerity, "The world was a better place because they were here!"

# 11

# *An Inspiration for Society*

△

The third function which salt had in the life of our Lord's society was that of making their very drab diet palatable. This condiment added a certain special tang to the simple food of the masses. Without it their regular ration of barley bread or roasted wheat cakes would have been well nigh unbearable for monotony.

We in the civilized Western world have almost no idea how drab and unexciting is the diet of millions upon millions of impoverished people throughout third world nations. Our enormous super markets, our fancy food service industry, our elaborate eating establishments, our extravagant life style of food consumption is a million miles removed from that of the masses living at subsistence levels.

Few of us are aware how terribly austere is a diet of rice—rice—rice every day in the year. Or how many of us have had to survive on nothing but corn meal—corn meal—corn meal month after month. What do we know about the grim, gaunt existence where only a handful of noodles or a scoop of potatoes or a crust of burned wheat loaf is all that stands between our empty, pinched stomachs and an early death by starvation?

The world in which I grew up as a small child was that kind of world. Before my father brought in better crops, better livestock, improved varieties of fruit and vegetables and poultry to lift the living standard of the Africans around us, most of them were undernourished. Almost all of them suffered severe symptoms of malnutrition. Few of them ever reached fifty years of age. A man or woman was old at forty, their bodies broken and diseased and misshapen from an inadequate diet.

In our part of the country corn meal, commonly referred to as *"posho,"* was the mainstay of the masses. This bland food, ground from the shriveled little kernels of their stunted corn cobs was consumed twice a day. The African ate at dawn, then again just after dusk. The corn meal *(posho)* was prepared either as a thin gruel or a sticky, thick mass of steaming hot material augmented with a few greens or, if very fortunate, occasionally a bit of meat.

But for all of them it was corn meal, corn meal, corn meal made palatable and edible and bearable only by the addition of salt. Without salt even the most sturdy native could not have endured such a severely Spartan fare. Only salt and perhaps once in a long while a spoonful of gravy could help them even swallow another mouthful of the monotonous diet.

A certain powerful, pensive pathos sweeps over my memories as I recollect those pioneer scenes. As a very small lad, the first job ever entrusted to me by my father was to spoon out a ration of salt from a huge cask of the condiment. Each African, who stood in line on Saturday afternoon awaiting his tiny share, was given the same quantity.

Government regulations on the frontier were that anyone who employed an African had to supply him/her with a daily ration of corn meal *(posho)* and a weekly supply of salt. It was an absolute imperative for their survival. And I still recall clearly how their hands would be extended eagerly to take this rare and delectable condiment. How they would flash their shining, white teeth if a few extra crystals spilled into their sweating palms. How they would berate me if they felt the spoon was not heaped quite high enough for a full ration.

Yes, salt was precious, special, and very significant in the stern simplicity of their life style. It made mere survival at least bearable.

Jesus knew all about this. He had lived, grown up and toiled among the common people of Palestine. He was intimately acquainted with the tough realities of trying to wrest a grim livelihood from a barren land that often produced very little. He had shared in the struggle to survive, the monotony of poor people's fare, the drabness of daily drudgery and the boredom of barely finding enough barley bread to fend off starvation.

Are we surprised that in His well-known and familiar prayer He asked, "Our Father, give us this day our daily bread"? He could easily have added, "seasoned with salt"! Yes, He was not far removed from all the stresses and strains of His society.

So turning to His disciples, and to you and me, He says: *"You are to be of similar service in society. You are to be that element which makes life bearable. You are to be the salt that brings zest and a tang to whatever it touches. Your life is to inject inspiration and enthusiasm into the drabness and boredom of the world in which you live."*

Though it is not commonly recognized, nor seldom ever publicly admitted, human society is burdened by boredom. Even in our sophisticated Western civilization with all of its emphasis on entertainment, leisure, pleasure and pastimes of a thousand sorts, people are pathetically bored. Somehow, in spite of our affluence, in spite of our education, in spite of our gadgetry and gimmicks, the general populace is woefully wearied by it all. For millions of individuals life is a drag.

During the intense years of my active ministry as a lay

pastor, it astonished me to see how often the root problem of people seeking spiritual help was one of basic boredom. In fact it was almost as difficult to get people to admit this as it was to have them confess they were sinners. Somehow no one likes to face the fact of his own tediousness. It is to admit missing the mark in life.

Yet all around us, especially in large metropolitan areas, millions of individuals live out their little days in quiet desperation. They are lonely, fearful and bored. In commenting on this common condition Jerome Frank declares: ". . . too many people today have too much money and not enough to do, and they turn to psychotherapy to combat the resulting boredom. It supplies novelty, excitement and, as a means of self-improvement(?), a legitimate way of spending money."

But beyond this, bored people turn to a hundred other pursuits and pastimes to try and inject some sort of spice into their drab days. They seek thrills, excitement and escape from the tedium that traps them amid their apparent affluence. Many of the masses who are mesmerized by the false philosophies of modern men little realize the drab despair of humanism, the utter emptiness of evolutionary philosophy, the dry-as-dust tedium of false teachings that take them nowhere without hope.

For all such our Lord comes along and says to us who know Him, *"You are the salt in this society. You are the ones who must introduce an element of hope, vitality, eagerness and exuberance into their lives. You must bring the zest that will make life bearable for them."*

This, of course, is only possible if and when it is the very life of the Risen, Resurrected Christ, who lives and moves and has His being in us. He it is who is not only the Savior of the world, but also the Savior for society, expressing Himself through us His people. It is His presence, His Spirit, His potency which can make a person's life palatable even under the most austere circumstances. It is He who alone brings that touch of optimism, the powerful pungency of hope, the delectable delight of divine life into our mundane world.

How then can and does this work out in our common little round of ordinary living? How can we in truth become salt to the sad, the lonely, the despairing, the jaded, the bored all about us?

Here are some simple yet potent suggestions.

## 1) Supply Encouragement

As Christians one of our hallmarks should be that of courage and fortitude. All through God's Word He gives us enormous encouragement (e.g. read Joshua 1). He exhorts us to take heart, to be strong, to be courageous.

Our late twentieth century society is notorious for its despair, its cynicsm. The media is in the control of skeptics. Gloom and doom are dispensed in large doses from books, magazines, newspapers, radio and T.V. programs.

As God's people we are to encourage those around us. We are to show them there can be purpose, direction, and fulfillment in life. Let us draw alongside the weak and faltering to lift their hearts, fire their hopes and transfer their attention from failing to our Father's faithfulness.

## 2) Bring Optimism to Others

God's people are realists. We recognize we are in a decadent society. We see corruption and decay everywhere. Yet amid the mayhem our spirits soar in hope. For our confidence is not in the community of man but in the goodness and graciousness of our God.

We are acutely aware of increasing anarchy. Yet we are intensely excited about the redemptive work of Christ rescuing men and women from the chaos.

We can challenge others to follow the Master. We can inspire them to serve God and serve men. We can look up and see the stars when others only look down and see the mud.

## 3) Contribute Comfort

All of us live amid a dying world. Death dominates the planet—not just physical death, but also the death of hopes, dreams, ambitions, love, family, friends and a hundred other human aspirations.

Yet in spite of all this decadence and despair life can be beautiful. We can bring comfort, cheer and consolation to our contemporaries. We can be those who weep with those who weep, who smile through the tears with those who smile through their tears.

We can draw near to help people pick up the pieces and make a fresh start. We can bring beauty for ashes. We can share the Spirit of God's joy to replace the spirit of a heavy heart.

## 4) Give Love

Not just soft sentimental affection, but the salty, strong, stringent love of a laid-down life. Give of your time, your thought, your attention, your care, your strength and your means to sharpen and excite the life of another.

Inject some unexpected surprise into the drab days of those less fortunate than you are. It will surprise you how your presence, your generosity, your acquaintance will be cherished and esteemed. You will not only be doing others a favor, but also yourself. Let your mind, your emotions, your will (heart), your hands, your feet, your lips, your eyes be Christ's in your world.

## 5) Be a Friend

It sounds old and perhaps stale, but lend a hand. Increasingly we live in a crowded society of solitary souls. People become ever more independent yet ever more grimly isolated amid our crowded communities.

In spite of all our emphasis on "togetherness" the general populace perishes in dreadful "apartness." The former filial bonds of brother and sister, child and parent, neighbor and neighbor are breaking down.

In daring concern and compassion let us reach out to befriend the friendless, to lend a touching hand, to lift a saddened soul despairing in lonesomeness.

We who really, truly, vitally know Christ as our closest Friend will feel constrained and compelled to extend that same friendship to those around us.

### 6) Inject Humor into Life

Wholesome fun, gaiety and good cheer are ever in short supply. Genuine hearty laughter does as much good as the finest medication.

So much social humor is snide and sarcastic. Fun is manufactured at the expense of others who suffer because of it. Scorn, ridicule and abuse is the world's way to get a hollow "belly laugh." But this is not God's way, nor the Christian's.

We can bring good cheer, good will and gaiety without undue levity. We can learn to see the funny side of even seeming debacles. We can inject a spirit of hope, humor and optimism into the most drab and difficult situations.

It takes self-control, discipline and a desire to lend relief in the midst of morbid men to do this. But the spirit sensitive to God's Spirit will know the appropriate moment when humor brings benefit.

### 7) Exercise Empathy

It takes time, thought and careful attention to the needs of others to put ourselves in their place, to see ourselves in their shoes, to hoe their row in life.

But when we do take this deep interest in them, God will use the door so opened to enter and enrich their experience, no matter how drab or desperate.

Let the Lord use you to enliven others. Let Him, at work in you, bring inspiration, beauty, uplift to the downcast.

From all sorts of people, from all over the world, letters come to my desk telling of the encouragement, the zest, the thrill, the stimulation brought to others by my books. This is a heartening thing both for them and me. I take no personal pride in it. This is the special work of the Spirit of God directing my writing, working with me. Yet it is salt for society.

# 12

# *For Healing of Others*

△

In the social life and culture of Christ's day salt played a most significant role in being the most common medication. Unlike our modern Western world, there simply were no elaborate pharmacies or handy drug stores standing on the street corners.

Even such common cures and medications as we now take for granted were utterly unknown then. The majority of medications were special herbs. And of all those household treatments used most often by the peasant people, common salt was by far the most handy remedy.

It was recognized from earliest times as an excellent sterilizing agency to prevent infection of wounds, open sores or abrasions. If a man were injured in battle, or a farmer gored by a bull, or a child bruised on arms and knees, a strong solution of salt water was used to cleanse and help the injury.

In the little white-washed dispensary where my mother and dad, in their simple service to sick Africans, attempted to tend their many illnesses, salt was a medication used much of the time. Warm water with salt dissolved in it was the disinfectant to cleanse ulcers or wash gaping knife and club wounds or sterilize the claw marks left by a mauling leopard.

As a boy I simply never knew anything but common salt as the powerful, pungent antidote for all the bruises and abrasions a growing lad suffers in his years of maturing into manhood. I can still recall clearly the enormous excitement produced in our home when the first bottles of Mercurochrome came into use. It did not burn and scald as salt did. And the Africans were quite sure it was the European's special, magic, healing blood because of its bright red color.

In those far-off frontier days salt was the material most of us who lived in the bush used to clean our teeth. There was no toothpaste readily available from brightly lit drug stores. So we simply used salt and it did an excellent job.

It was the same for colds, coughs and sore throats. A strong salt solution was used to gargle with regularly. It cleared up the condition as quickly as the most highly advertised and expensive medications do today.

We young, eager, energetic hunters in search of game to provide meat for the table would even flick a tiny pinch of salt into our eyes to clear our vision and sharpen our sight. Nor did any of these apparently crude and simple uses of this common element do us any harm. Rather the opposite, for at well over sixty years of age I still have my own teeth and require no glasses for reading or other close work.

In my biographical book, *Bold under God,* now published under the new title, *A Fond Look at a Frontier Preacher,* I tell the story of how Mr. Charles Bowen saved all the lives of the people who were rescued from the torpedoed liner *Athenia* in World War II. This was the first passenger ship sunk by the German U-Boats in fierce conflict.

After the survivors were picked up by another ship which came to the rescue, all medical supplies were quickly exhausted. There were so many bruised, wounded and shattered bodies on board that the resourceful Mr. Bowen could do nothing more than have them all bathed regularly with salt water drawn up in buckets from the sea.

Though this seemed a crude way to care for the injured invalids, not a single passenger perished. All of them were able to reach port alive and there receive further medical aid. So the role of salt was the key to their very survival from a nightmare ordeal at sea.

Jesus and His men knew all about this significant use of salt as a means of healing. And when He looked tenderly at His twelve, tough young companions and said: *"You are the salt of the earth!"* He meant it in this role as well.

The profound prophetic predictions made in the Old Testament regarding the coming of Christ, cast Him in the role of a healer. He—"The Messiah," "The Anointed One of God," "The Comforter"—would come to bind up the brokenhearted; to mend the bruised; to restore the injured; to raise the sick; to bring healing to the hurt.

> The spirit of the Lord God
> is upon me; because the Lord
> hath anointed me to preach good
> tidings unto the meek;
> he hath sent me to bind up
> the brokenhearted, to proclaim
> liberty to the captives,
> and the opening of the prison to
> them that are bound (Isa. 61:1).

So there comes home to us today, just as it did in our Lord's day, that we are to be those who somehow help to heal our sick and suffering society. It was pointed out in the first part of this book that we have a society suffering from terminal illness. Yet amid all of its maladies we are called to make a contribution that will help in its recovery.

I would here like to remind the reader again that the

118 △ SALT FOR SOCIETY

reason salt was such an excellent remedy was due to its peculiar pungency, its diametrical difference, its unique qualities that set it apart from that to which it was applied. The sharper its "bite," the more pronounced its potency, the more effective its healing qualities.

If salt had lost its savor, if it was bland, if it no longer carried a powerful pungency, it was of little or no use as a distinct healing agent. The same is true of God's people. We simply have to be distinct; we have to be different; we have to be readily distinguished to help heal our world.

There is no inherent merit in being "different" just to be different. There is no significant use in being odd or noticeable just to attract attention. There is no need for us to be "queer" characters.

Christ calls us to be among men. He urges us to penetrate and permeate the world of our generation. He asks us to lose ourselves in serving our sick society. But in all of this it is the uniqueness of His life in us which ultimately contributes to the healing of those whose lives we touch. It is not our personal peculiarity.

Our difference is not in our egocentricity, but rather our potency must be our Christ-centeredness. It is not me who heals broken hearts, broken homes, broken hopes, broken harmony, it is He, Christ in me. It is God expressing Himself through my human personality who brings blessing and benefit to a broken world.

This "healing" of which I speak is not something I seek to do for my own self-gratification or self-aggrandizement. As a Christian, I do not parade my piety as a means of personal fulfillment. Helping to heal sinful society is not something undertaken to undergird my own self-esteem. I do not become a "do-gooder" to garner glory to myself.

Rather the emphasis is that we are amid the sick and suffering. We move among all sorts and conditions of men who are injured and broken in the battles of life. We live amid death. So in our living we are called of Christ to be that special element that without fanfare or ostentation does its beautiful work of binding up the broken.

Modern Christianity is much, much too preoccupied with the spectacular, the sensational, the dramatic. We of the Western world with our "success syndrome" seem to insist that God's work in the world has to be big, bold and brash. We are too eager to wave our arms, blow our bugles and broadcast our brand of belief to attract attention on the earth.

Salt does not work that way. It is a substance that silently, quietly does its work with enormous effectiveness.

Here are some helpful suggestions for us to be salt in healing our society.

We need to see that God our Father wishes to heal the whole person. Man is more than just a physical being. He is also more than just a soul with mind, emotions and will. He is more than just a spirit with spiritual needs. He is all of these.

We do society a distinct disservice in assuming that its ill can be cured by treating only one or two of its affected parts. Too many Christians glibly crusade all their lives on the premise that man's problems are only spiritual. They simply are not!

When our Lord was here, he demonstrated unmistakably and without question that He was concerned with all of life. Not only did He forgive men and women their sins, but also He healed their sicknesses, fed their bodies, brought comfort to the emotionally distraught, cast out evil spirits, and built better tables and beds.

It has been stated before in this book, yet it cannot be overemphasized here again, that as Christ's followers we are to make our contribution to the well-being of our world no matter where we live or whatever our work.

In God's economy and in His estimation, there is no sharp distinction between secular and sacred work. Man makes much of special "ministries." It has well-nigh become a mania among many Christians. There is an element of pride and prestige attached to certain professional roles in the Christian community.

This is not our Lord's view of us being salt. He is not impressed with those who go around shouting, "Lord, Lord! In Your name we preached; we prophesied; we did many miracles; we worked great works!"

Rather, He is looking for the faithful, quiet, trustworthy soul who simply does His work well in the world. The one who quietly carries out His wishes, earns a grand "well done."

This work of "healing" can take a thousand different forms. This book cannot begin to list or enumerate all the ways in which God's people can "turn around" the terminal illness of our society.

We are told very clearly in 1 Corinthians 12:28 that God's gracious Spirit gives to many of us the gifts of healing, the gifts of help. And these can be of a hundred sorts.

The intelligent farmer who conserves his soil, improves his pastures, raises nourishing crops and better livestock to feed a starving world is helping to relieve the world's pain just as surely as the cancer specialist who applies cobalt radiation to a patient's malignant tumor alleviates his illness. The contractor who builds better homes for less money and with more efficient use of energy is healing some of society's sickness just as surely as the preacher who calls for repentance from the pulpit. The mother who raises healthy, happy, well-adjusted children is helping to heal society as much as the social worker who struggles to bring better conditions to the underprivileged of the ghetto.

All of us together as God's children can be "healers." We don't have to be hucksters peddling cheap remedies to the gullible masses. We don't need to indulge in spectacular campaigns and "special services" to right all the wrongs in our wretched world.

We of the west want too much "sudden" success. We are looking for massive miracles. We want "instant" cures.

We search frantically for fantastic programs that will capture the attention of the whole wide world.

Jesus was content to quietly introduce twelve of His companions to a "different" life style of giving themselves wholeheartedly in service to others. He never once asked them to be successful. He never once insisted that they should be spectacular people. He never suggested that they be flashy or flamboyant. He just encouraged them to be faithful.

The peculiar property of salt as a "healing" agent is that when applied to a wound or bruise, it quickly penetrates the problem area, then disappears. The same principle should apply to us. We are too often unwilling to lose ourselves in helping to heal. We are too determined to preserve our special identity; we want somehow to be very much "seen," acknowledged and given special credit for our contribution.

Professor Henry Drummond in one of his remarkable essays makes the statement that true Christianity, true love, true "selflessness" does its own delightful healing, saving work in secret. Then it steals away in silence, unseen, forgetting even its own lowly, winsome touch upon the life of another.

Our Lord made much of this principle in His teaching. He pointed out the unnoticed widow who gave all she had in her two tiny mites of money. He told the story of the poor, contrite publican praying unheard, unseen in his quiet corner. He recounted the stirring saga of the shepherd who alone, unsung, in the wilderness, rescued one wandering sheep. These were His heroes. These were the "great" ones in His estimation who by the world's standards were second-rate people.

Salt is not showy! Salt is not spectacular! Salt is not strident! It is simple. It is silent. Yet it is special in its healing qualities.

Only rarely, here and there, does God ever call a man or woman to special display or dramatic demonstrations.

Much more often He simply asks us to be those silent, sincere souls who in service to Him and those around us help to heal a hurting, broken world.

We can bring to this sick world honest work, inspiring hope, good cheer, lofty ideals, a helping hand, a warm heart, a shining smile, a word of encouragement, a friendly hug, a share of ourselves.

Because we have been here some broken heart, some broken home or some broken hope will have been healed. And even God will be glad.

# 13

## For Benefiting All Who Serve

△

During the life of our Lord, a considerable proportion of the population were peasants who lived on the land. All of those who tilled the soil, grew crops, or carried on trade or transport used livestock as a source of power.

Oxen, camels and donkeys could be seen everywhere. They were used to plow the fields, harrow the clods and haul loads. The poorest peasant owned some livestock, while the richer noblemen had lovely estates with stables of camels or horses.

Caravans crisscrossed the countryside bearing articles of trade and commerce from one community to another. Everywhere one went livestock were seen at work carrying goods, thrashing grain, pumping water, working the land, bearing people on their backs.

There were no cars, no trucks, no trains, no aircraft, not even a bicycle for a boy to ride. All business, barter, commerce, agriculture and local transportation depended entirely on animal strength.

Jesus knew all about this. As He worked so carefully and skillfully in the carpenter shop, fixing broken plows, building strong wooden harrows, making smooth, comfortable yokes for beasts of burden, His clients would chat to Him about their simple, hearty life on the land.

Over and over they would tell the genial, strong carpenter all about the care of their animals. They would remind Him how hard and expensive it was to find enough fodder or grain for their oxen, donkeys, camels or horses. Always, too, they came around to the subject of salt. All their livestock simply had to have salt if they were to be fit and strong for service.

Procuring salt for animals was not nearly as easy as it is now. The large square blocks of salt we find on every farm and ranch today where animals are kept, simply did not exist in those early days. Instead the people had to take time out to drive their stock long distances to natural "mineral licks." These were places where outcroppings of salt and minerals occurred in the broken terrain. Or it might be the edge of a salt marsh or "salt pan" where, through evaporation, a layer of salt was left lying on the edge. There animals could pick it up.

In the plains and hills of East Africa where I spent twenty years of my life, salt licks were special spots. Often they were found deep down in the dongas where an exposed bank of earth had been licked smooth by uncounted thousands of domestic and wild animals for centuries. I have followed the well-worn trails cut deep through solid sandstone by the passing to and fro of animals searching for salt.

Salt was just as essential for their survival as for ours. Jesus was aware of this too. He knew that salt was one of the major keys to the well-being of all the lowly livestock engaged in service to men.

So when He looked calmly into the questioning eyes of His eager young associates, He had this concept in mind as well: *"You are the salt of the earth. You are to be that element in society that invigorates all of those engaged in service to us."*

This all seems so very simple. Yet it is distinctly surprising how few of us really play this role properly as the people of God.

Let me illustrate. Just recently my wife and I visited in the home of a young lady who has become a splendid singer and outstanding music teacher. She was telling us of the years she served as a waitress in small restaurants, earning a few dollars to pay for her music lessons. They were difficult and discouraging days. Not being strong or robust she would be totally exhausted and ready to collapse by the end of her shift.

She stated that the hardest part of the job was to be more or less ignored by the customers, to be taken for granted, to be treated as though she was just another piece of equipment in the place.

She was saying how much it meant to her in that menial job if the customers would just look in her eyes, acknowledge she too was a person and perhaps pass her a smile or some simple compliment.

What she was saying in so many words was that she who served also needed the spice and sparkle of a bit of salt in her austere life. How many of us really do this for those who serve us? How many of us are willing to be selfless enough in our fleeting contacts with other human beings to bring the stimulation of encouragement to their often drab and tedious duties?

We are all served by one another. Even the President or Prime Minister of a nation serves. The civil servants in a thousand departments, bureaus and offices serve us, as do the clerks in stores, the people at gas pumps and garages, the policemen, the postmen, the delivery boys, the airline stewardesses, the pilots, the engineers. All of us everywhere in society, no matter what our career may be, either directly or indirectly, serve each other.

Do we really see this? Do we use our contacts with each other to lighten their load, lift their spirits, encourage their best efforts, show our genuine gratitude for their service?

It takes so little to do so much great good in this weary old world. Just a fleeting but sincere smile and word of thanks can make the whole day bright for a working person. A note of thanks dropped in the mail expressing appreciation, a phone call to compliment another, a hearty handshake to show good will, these are things all of us can offer.

If we are to be salt in society as Christians, this unique and wondrous quality of genuine gratitude and hearty appreciation should mark all of our actions and activities in interpersonal relationships. We should be known for the tang and zest we bring to those whose lives we touch.

During the years that I served as a lay pastor to various congregations, it came home to me with enormous force how precious "salty" people were. In any congregation there are the chronic complainers. No matter how well the work went, no matter how richly God was pleased to bless His people, no matter how sweet and cordial the fellowship, some could always find fault.

Yet on the other hand there were also those dear, dear souls who took time to uplift, cheer, encourage and hearten the pastor who served them. Some of us do not realize that the word *minister* means "to serve." Our ministers are our servants, not our masters. But we in turn, as those served, need to be the salt in their lives and experience, that spurs them on to ever more noble service to God and men.

A pastor's role in the late twentieth century is one of the most demanding and difficult careers any person can enter. The days are gone when a minister's congregation was composed of solid, stable families who were staunch and steadfast in their loyalty to the church. Today at least 20 percent of the population moves every year. Congregations are in flux. Families are fragmented. Old values and standards of behavior collapse. And those who minister amid the chaos of society are inundated day after day, and night after night, with the burdens of a broken world.

Only the person who has been a caring pastor can begin to comprehend the heartache, the despair, the deep discouragement endured by a staggering society sinking in sin. Such a one needs and must have relief and good cheer from the salty Christians in his congregation. He must hear about their triumphs, their successes, their victories. He needs to know that not all is dark and despondent. He needs to have some of his people share their homes, their happiness, their humor, their hearty encouragement with him, so he, too, can carry on in strength.

Do you do this? If so, you are salt for society.

There are one or two aspects to this sort of simple service that need to be explained here. They can very well change the whole complexion of a person's character.

First it does take a little extra time to live with an attitude of gratitude in our contacts with others. As the old, well loved hymn puts it, "Take time to be holy." That means "wholesome, well rounded, helpful."

It takes time to stop a minute or two and thank a clerk, a waiter, a gardener, and office employee for the work they have done well.

But if we are people meek and humble in heart, we will make the time to do this. We will find spare moments in which to write a short note of appreciation. We will set time aside to call people and compliment them on the contribution they have made.

Long ago someone said this is what it means "to have an educated heart." This is what it means to be sensitive to the needs of another. This is what it means to be salt to those who serve.

In my own present careers as an author, speaker and Bible teacher, it is a constant source of good cheer and genuine enthusiasm to recieve encouragement from those who read the books or attend the lectures or sit in the Bible studies. This is to be heartened in the work by those who take time to express their appreciation. It is wondrous to know our Father has used the book or message or study to touch some other life. It is a joy to be reminded again of His faithfulness. It is a thrill to see people respond to the overtures of Christ. It is a powerful incentive to press on when we see God's gracious Spirit at work in the world.

But this can happen only when people take the time and thought to express themselves in words spoken or written. And to all such "salty" people I have always felt deeply indebted and joyfully grateful.

The second aspect to this role of being salt in society is that it does demand genuine selflessness on our part. Put another way, we might well say that we in turn become servants to those who serve.

Not only does it take time, it takes concentration of thought and genuine interest in another. It means I must set aside my own immediate interests and self-preoccupation to put myself in the other person's place. It means I try to enter into their experience so that I can have empathy for their role in life.

Often when I am standing in line waiting for service, either at a post office wicket, a bank teller's cage, or a check-out counter I try to imagine the terrible tedium and constant pressure of serving the public in such a stringent situation. By the time my turn comes, I endeavor to bring a word of good will, a humorous remark or a gentle compliment that will lighten the clerk's work load for that day. They, too, are human. They, too, need help. They, too, will be encouraged by my passing that way.

This, as far as I can understand it, is the fine, stimulating, strengthening, service that we as God's people can render to those who serve. Let us not take others for granted. Let us not be dull to their drudgery. Let us not be insensitive to their suffering.

We can be salt for society. We can be those who bless our contemporaries. We can be great people in small ways. Read carefully: Philippians 2:1-9.

Too often in Christian circles there is a tendency to think that to be effective we must be big or conspicuous or outstanding in our service to society. Not so! That may be the world's way, but it is not necessarily God's way.

It has always impressed me how our Lord when He was here serving people, repeatedly told them to go home quietly and not publicize the miracles He had performed for them. He was not seeking notoriety. He was not eager to be acclaimed. He was not keen to be in the limelight. He just went about calmly, gently, doing good.

Much of the energy, time and thought which we in the West devote to programs, if invested directly and individually in friends, acquaintances and family, would alter the entire complexion of our communities. We are too preoccupied with the "big plans" rather than the "little people" all around us.

If you are a husband, when was the last time you cared enough to stop and give your wife genuine gratitude for a meal she prepared? If you are a wife, when have you been thoughtful enough to congratulate your husband on putting up with the stresses and strains of his work to provide a home and income for you? When as a parent have you written your child a letter complimenting him/her on their achievements? What thought and appreciation have you shown your parents for all the sacrifice endured to assure your success in life?

All of us take each other too much for granted. It is a deadening, dulling, destructive habit. God calls us to care. He calls us to see with knowing eyes. He calls us to detect with sensitivity the heart needs of those around us. Our response can be one of enormous benefit and blessings, not in some grandiose performance, but in a hundred little helping ways.

We can be salt to our associates. We can bring zest, fun, vitality, love and light to their lives. We can enliven their drab days.

# 14

## *For Loyalty and Friendship*

△

The sixth significant role of salt in the culture of New Testament times was one of winsome symbolism. This precious commodity, which was so essential in the lives of the common people, also represented those rare and lofty qualities of loyalty and friendship so necessary for human well-being.

There is no doubt whatever that our Lord had this role in mind for His men. When He looked into their burning, bright, eager eyes and declared without hesitation: "You are the salt of the earth!" He meant it in the sense of steadfastness, strength and trustworthiness.

Only those of us who have lived and grown up in the social milieu of the East fully appreciate the appalling sort of society into which Jesus, the Christ, was born. Deceit and graft and lying were all an accepted way of life. Honesty, integrity, fidelity and genuine loyalty were rare qualities, seldom if ever encountered in the life of the people.

In fact, it was considered "clever" to be able to deceive and mislead others in order to gain advantage. Craftiness, cunning and outright cheating were cruel games practiced by most of the people. Outright, rank dishonesty was a part of everyday life.

This is why Jesus, who declared Himself to be "the truth," was so hated and abused. It explains the ferocious encounters He had with the scribes and Pharisees whom He so often charged with lying. It helps us to understand why He placed such a premium on integrity, on the credibility of human conduct, on a man's "yes" being "yes," and his "no" being "no."

Yet amid all this social malaise there remained a beautiful, social custom referred to as "eating the king's salt," or sometimes called, "sharing a friend's salt."

If people were given opportunity to visit the town or city where nobility lived, on rare occasions they might be invited to a banquet or social function arranged for special guests. At such festive occasions new friendships were formed. And if the local chief, lord, prince, ruler or even possibly monarch, felt attracted to a certain guest, that one would be invited to partake of "the king's salt."

A small, ornamental saucer, containing a spoonful of salt, would be placed before the new acquaintance. That person would then be invited to take a pinch of the salt with his fingers and place it on his tongue. By partaking of the host's salt in this way, the guest indicated in unmistakable language that he/she reciprocated the friendship and accord between the two people.

But beyond this, taking and tasting "the king's salt" had the profound symbolism of binding the two people into an unbreakable pact of loyalty and fidelity. To eat salt in this way was to indicate publicly that a bond of friendship and life-long devotion has been formed between the two parties.

Salt played precisely the same role in the life of the common people, between friend and friend. Instead of representing allegiance between people of lower and higher rank as with perhaps a commoner and chieftain, it was the guarantee of unbroken comradeship between those of similar social standing.

In short, salt was the well-known, well-respected, well-understood denoter of trustworthiness between people. It stood for integrity and truth. It stood for trust and loyalty so essential for friendships and fidelity in the fragmented family of man.

This Jesus knew well. This His disciples grasped clearly. And this He intends we should be in our role as His people in a broken world and shattered society.

In this setting we must ask ourselves some very hard questions.

Do I live a credible life?

Am I genuine? Or do I play games?

Can I be counted on to "come through"?

Is my "yes," "yes," and my "no," "no"?

Does my behavior foster loyalty and friendship?

These are not spectacular things to do. There is nothing sensational about being solid and reliable. It is not the sort of conduct to be acclaimed by the media, or even other people.

But it is this element of quiet integrity and loyal fidelity that the Master looks for among His followers. In this dimension we should be sharply and pungently distinct from our contemporaries. We need to be known and recognized as people of "our word." What we say we mean. How we behave declares our deepest intentions and reveals our true inner attitudes.

It is all very well to make lofty statements of this sort either on a written page or from a podium. It is infinitely more difficult to live them out in the common round of our daily contact with other human beings. Our culture conditions us to live behind a false façade of geniality. We are sophisticated to the point where we can pretend to be other than we are. Our civilized cynicism leads many "to smile in your face while slitting your jugular vein."

Judas was by no means the last double dealer who embraced and kissed his friend while scheming to destroy Him. This treacherous trait of breaking bonds of loyalty, of injuring those who trust us, of betraying those who count on our comradeship is not peculiar only to primitive people. It is rampant everywhere. It ravages the whole of society.

Not only do nations, empires, and governments break their written agreements and signed compacts, but so, also, do the little people in their everyday lives. Business "deals," industrial contracts are nullified with impunity, but then so, too, are marriage contracts and bonds of fidelity between friends.

Men and women charge and counter charge each other with duplicity and double dealing. The lawyers and solicitors (so-called) wax fat on the ever-increasing litigation of fragmented family life. Men and women who this week declare their undying allegiance to each other next week are walking out on each other.

The basic elements of loyalty and friendship become increasingly scarce in our society. It matters not whether this be toward a fellow human being, one's family, a society, the church, one's country or God Himself.

On every hand we see fragmentation rather than fidelity. We see the disintegration of what should be deep and meaningful relationships and how those involved are shaken and shattered in the trauma of our times. People look for someone to trust and are often taunted in their empty quest.

Amid all this mayhem Christ calls us to be salt for our society. He insists that we can be that element in a fragmented world which contributes to consistency and credibility. He looks to us as God's people who can be counted on to come through.

By saying this I am not advocating grandiose schemes or impressive programs wherein the so-called "piety" is paraded to attract public attention. Far too often such spectacles are less than honest and do much more damage than good. Witness the dubious role of people in public life, or in the media, who make so much of their honesty or integrity only to deceive and disappoint their admirers.

What is here being advocated is that essential trustworthiness that expresses itself in all of our daily duties and interpersonal relationships. Let us make our "yes," "yes." Let us be sure our "no" is "no." Let us keep our promises. Let us carry out our commitments. Let us be reliable and resolute in our behavior.

If we say we will phone—then let us phone.
If we say we will write—then let us write.
If we say we will meet—then let us meet.
If we say we will do a job—then let us do it.
If we say we will pray—then let us pray.
If we say we will give—then let us give.
If we say we will love—then let us love.

In recent years it has astonished me again and again to have people remark to me with utter amazement, "You did what you said you would! " "You did write, you did phone, you did come, you did help, you did deliver!"

This simple, straightforward, solid reliability in the daily deportment of a Christian will do more to foster and generate fidelity in others than all the preaching of a lifetime. Not only will it encourage our contemporaries to put confidence in us, but much more importantly it will lead them, eventually, to meet the Master and put their trust in Him.

If in truth and in fact Christ does live in us by His gracious Spirit, His life will be expressed in basic honesty amid a crooked and corrupt society.

For it is God which worketh
in you both to will and to do
of his good pleasure.
Do all things without
murmurings and disputings:
that ye may be blameless and harmless,
the sons of God, without rebuke,
in the midst of a crooked and perverse
nation, among whom ye shine as lights
in the world (Phil. 2:13–15).

Sincerity and integrity may not be the most glamorous qualities sought after by our society. Yet if it is to survive at all, if it is to be saved from ultimate decadence, if it is to be restored to some semblance of its former greatness, truth and fidelity must flourish again.

And this is possible only if these qualities first find genuine expression in the lives of God's people.

It is in this connection that I would here give great credit to the essential integrity of the character of Christ. Perhaps as a rough, rather rugged man, no other single attribute in the life of our Lord has drawn me to Him with such enormous impetus.

It is the strength of His honesty, it is the total trustworthiness of His character, it is the utter credibility of His commitments to me that have drawn and bound my wild, willful, wayward spirit to Himself with bonds of steel.

He is in truth and in fact my fondest friend. He is in living reality my most loyal companion amid a chaotic society. He is the precious person, deeply appreciated, who is ever "the perfect gentleman" because of His impeccable, unfailing conduct toward me.

God, my Father, all through a long and exciting life has never betrayed me. He has never deceived me. He has never double-crossed me. Any tiny fragment of faith and confidence ever invested in Him, He has always honored. He has made good on all His commitments to me as a common man. What greater confidence can one find today than to walk in company with such a companion?

So it is that something of that comradeship and association with God's Spirit should express itself in my spirit. It need not be stunning; it need not be sensational. But it does need to be so sincere that others will see and know that I walk with God, and He with me.

In this there is more help for a shaky society than in ten thousand stuffy sermons.

# 15

# *For Sacrifice and Suffering*

△

The seventh significant function which salt had in the culture of our Lord's time had to do with the offering of sacrifices and oblations to God. This was an ancient practice that had been performed for some 1500 years by the people of Israel.

> As for the oblation of the Firstfruits,
> ye shall offer them unto the Lord:
> but they shall not be burnt on the altar
> for a sweet savor.
> and every oblation of thy meat offering
> shalt thou season with salt;
> neither shalt thou suffer the salt of
> the covenant of thy God to be lacking
> from thy meat offering:
> with all thine offerings thou shalt offer
> salt (Lev. 2:12–13).

This special Levitical edict, given by Moses to his people, was one observed with meticulous care by all those who at any time, in any place, offered meat and burnt offerings to Jehovah. Jesus knew all about this ordinance, and so did His disciples. He was as familiar with this peculiar rite as all His contemporaries.

It was the duty and serious responsibility of the common people to see to it that all the sons of Levi, the specially appointed priesthood in Israel, were supplied regularly with a ration of salt. Because they offered large numbers of slaughtered beasts, both lambs and bullocks in sacrifice, the quantities of salt consumed in these religious rites were enormous.

It may well be asked why salt was considered to be an essential ingredient of the meat offering. Flesh, when consumed on an open fire, emits a repulsive, rather disagreeable odor. In fact, for some it is almost nauseating. But when salt is rubbed into the raw flesh, then exposed to the heat and flames, it gives off a peculiar, pleasant, sweet savor (aroma). This was the unique and essential role of the element in the sacrifice.

Of course each part of the sacrifice bore with it a special significance well understood by both the priest and the penitent. All the Old Testament offerings of lambs and bullocks were but a looking forward to the supreme sacrifice of God's own Lamb, His Son, our Savior at Calvary. The millions of humble sacrifices offered upon thousands of altars across fifteen centuries of human history were a continuous foreshadowing of Christ's sublime offering of Himself as our substitute in His own death.

The significance of the salt itself in these rites was that it in turn represented the self-giving of the donor. Any poor, wretched man or woman who in contrition of heart and brokenness of spirit brought a sacrificial beast for sacrifice, brought also his or her salt for deliberate self-identification with the offering.

Just as the flesh was to be completely consumed by the fire, so too was the salt. Just as the meat burned up in the blaze stood as a substitute for the Savior, so the salt stood as a substitute for the sinner. Flesh and salt together comprised a complete and satisfactory oblation, a sweet savor to God. Both together provided the perfect propitiation for any wrongs done, and any sins staining the life.

The deep, stirring, sensitive explanation of this principle is clearly declared by the apostle Paul in his remarkable letter to the church at Rome. Read Romans 6:5–14 with great care.

Our Lord knew all about this too. So did His men. In so many words He was saying to them, *"You, as salt, are to have this same sacrificial role in society!"*

Repeatedly throughout the Word of God, our Lord Jesus Christ is depicted for us by God's gracious Spirit as the suffering Savior. He is shown to us as the suffering Servant (Phil. 2:1–10). He is pictured in profoundly stirring phrases as the Man of Sorrows acquainted with grief (Isa. 53).

This One, this God, our God, was prepared to set aside all of His celestial splendor and power to enter human history. In total identification with us in our common humanity He endured incredible condescension and unimaginable abuse at human hands.

What for?

Was it just a passing performance?

Was it merely to provide a model for us?

No, a thousand times no! It was to save us from our sins, to save us from our selves, to save us from Satan the enemy of our souls.

There simply was no other way.

The supreme sacrifice of Himself was essential for our total redemption and restoration to His family. And so it is He calls us in turn to become totally identified with Him in this suffering. He calls us to commit ourselves in self-giving, both to God and to other people. He calls us to "lose ourselves" in Him, just as salt loses itself in the sacrifice.

If society is to be redeemed, if men and women are to be saved, if atonement is to be made between God and men, then we have our part to play in the great redemptive purposes of Christ. We, too, as Christians must be fully prepared to be offered up in sacrifice. This is no easy thing. Most of us shun it. We prefer more pleasant activities.

The whole principle of new life springing up out of death is one which Jesus dealt with again and again. But in His day, as in ours, few fully understood.

He spoke emphatically about those who chose to follow Him. He stated categorically that they would have to deny themselves (give up, sacrifice their own rights), take up their crosses and follow Him to their own crucifixion.

The Christian is the person prepared to be wiped out in order that others may be salvaged. He is the individual daring enough to die that others may live. He is willing to lose himself that others may be found for the Master.

This sort of challenge has never appealed to the majority of people. Most human beings much prefer to be pandered to by their contemporaries. They seek the place of prominence and recognition. They love to bask in the limelight of public acclaim.

Yet Jesus said that if a person tried to spare his own life, pad his own comfortable nest, swathe himself in security and affluence, he was bound to lose it all.

Why?

Simply because anything we horde and save for ourselves is completely and forever forfeited to someone else, either God or man. We really only gain forever that which we give away in generosity with a glad hand. It is the seed buried in the darkness of the soil that bursts its bonds and leaps into new life of reproductive power. The seed kept securely, safely in a sack abides ever wrapped up all alone within its own shell until consumed by weevils or its own inner decay.

If as Christians in a crazy, chaotic society, we would be of service, we must be prepared to lay down our lives for others. This is not pious pap. This is the tough, strong, formidable force of the love of God at work in the world, through us.

The venerable apostle John put it this way in his lovely letter to Christians:

> Hereby perceive we the love of God, because he laid down his life for us: and we ought to lay down our lives for the brethren (1 John 3:16).

This is not some sweet sentimental emotion in which we indulge ourselves from time to time. It is the tough, abrasive task of tramping the trails of life with sorrow, self-sacrifice, tears and inner anguish—not because we are pious prudes, but because we are surrounded on every side with lost souls sinking in sin and darkness and despair.

In His all-knowing goodness, wisdom, compassion and mercy, God our Father calls all sorts of people to minister to all sorts of human need. Part of the great glory of the church is the capacity of Christians to meet the desperate demands of all sorts and conditions of men and women from all strata of society.

There are the "Mother Teresas " who "do something beautiful for God" amid the poorest of the poor in Calcutta.

There are the "Dave Wilkersons" who reclaim the dreadful drug addicts in the ghettos of New York.

There are the "Charles Colsons" who minister to the fierce, tough prison inmates.

There are the "Francis Schaeffers" who reach the elite intelligentsia of our day, so far astray in their sophistication.

In His own special, wondrous way, God our Father calls each of us to serve that segment of society where our particular background, experience, personality and training can be given in glad service. He does not ask us to try and save the whole of society. He does not suggest that any one of us can do it all. What He does require is that we be faithful where we are. He asks us to be alert and open to those

who cross our paths. He invites us to lay down our lives
for those immediately at hand.

An in-depth study of the life of Christ will make the above
principles very clear. When He was here among us as a
man, He simply did not attempt to be everywhere. He did
not try to go everywhere. He did not spread Himself so
thin He was of no use anywhere.

Instead He concentrated His time, His strength, His attention upon those particular people whose lives He touched.
Sometimes it would be a crowd. Sometimes it was only
His twelve disciples. Sometimes it was only a single soul
with whom He spoke.

We, too, like Him, live in a changing world. We live amid
all sorts of cultures. We are confronted with all classes and
conditions of men. There will be times when we speak to
large congregations. There will be occasions when we confer
only with a small, special group. There will be those intimate
moments of communing on a one-to-one basis.

All of this takes time. It calls for the expenditure of enormous energy. It requires a willingness to be totally available
to others. It entails self-sacrifice. It means we must be willing
to set aside our own self-interests to serve others. It demands
laying down our lives for others.

This is the noble, high, special life to which Christ calls
His followers. It will not be easy, but it can be exciting. It
will not be cozy, but it can be very creative. It will not be
noticed by one's contemporaries (except for a few famous
cases), but it will be taken note of by our Father.

Salt always penetrates, permeates and preserves that to
which it is applied. And we are called to precisely the same
severe service in our suffering for society. We do not look
for the easy spot. We do not search for self-realization or
self-fulfillment. We do not strive for public recognition or
accolades from our fellows. We dare not even expect appreciation—it seldom, if ever, comes from those for whom we
suffer.

We simply go out to love a dying world because it was initially God who first loved us.

We lay down our lives for others because Christ laid down His life for us.

We go out to lift and cheer and restore because in wondrous care and compassion God's gracious Spirit does this for us.

Our entire motivation in suffering for our generation is not to be a martyr, not to be a hero or heroine, not to be idolized by others, but to be identified with Christ in His suffering, to share our entire lives with others as He has shared His life with us.

Ultimately we must see and understand that all of this is only possible if indeed it is *Christ* who is actually alive and active in our life and experience. "It is God who worketh in you, both to will and to do of his good pleasure" (Phil. 2:13).

Then my life, my service, my suffering combined with His, becomes a sweet, pungent savor to both God and men— salt for society!

# 16

# *A Postscript for Salt*

△

It would be quite wonderful if this book could just end on the positive theme of the preceding chapter. But to be true to our Lord's discussion of salt with His men on the mount it cannot.

And for our own sakes it must not.

For the Master warned His listeners that salt having lost its pungency was still a potent, though very negative compound.

". . . If the salt have lost his savour, wherewith shall it be salted? It is thenceforth good for nothing but to be cast out, and to be trodden under foot of men" (Matt. 5:13).

Not many people comprehend clearly what was meant by this startling statement.

The peculiar property of salt is that even though it may have lost its pungency, its piquancy, it still retains one very devastating potency. This rare and remarkable material can still sterilize soil. It can destroy all plant life on the land. It can kill every blade of grass, green herb and tender shoot that tries to spring from salt-poisoned soil.

In ancient times before the advent of asphalt, concrete or mechanically crushed rock which are used now for road surfacing, salt was spread on roads and paths where people passed to and fro. Not only did it prevent the growth of all plant life, so keeping the roadway clear, but its capacity to absorb moisture compacted the surface under passing feet. The end result was utter bareness.

In time of war ancient adversaries used salt to insure the total devastation of captured towns or cities. After the people had been captured, the community plundered, valuables carried away and the buildings burned by fire, the remaining desolation would be to sow the land with salt. This meant the site where the city stood was left a desperate, barren wasteland where nothing could ever be grown again. The soil was totally sterilized, unfit to produce crops, fruit or even meager pasturage for uncounted years to come (see Judges 9:44–45).

All my life I have been an enthusiastic gardener. Wherever I have lived, in various countries throughout the world, it has always been a special pleasure to plant and tend gardens of flowers and vegetables and fruits. Winding in and out among these plantings have been little paths and walkways. Always, the means used to keep them clear and free of weeds, grass and undesirable growth was to scatter coarse salt upon them. It is effective, inexpensive yet deadly.

This is the effect Jesus had in mind when He warned His followers that even in its most undesirable condition this condiment was still capable of having a pronounced negative impact.

Put in another way, we can say that salt, whether pungent or not, is still able to kill and destroy that to which it is applied. In seven out of the eight uses the results are positive, exceedingly beneficial and healthful. The eighth use conversely is negative and ends only in barrenness.

Precisely the same principle applies in the case of the Christian. Either our lives are counting for good and for

God or they are making an impact for evil and the enemy of our souls.

The way we live, the things we say, the attitudes we entertain, the life style we adopt, the enterprises in which we engage are all continuously producing either positive or negative results in society. Far too many people assume they can adopt a neutral stance. They feel they can be noncommittal. They try to remain detached, uninvolved with the trauma, turmoil and tension of their times.

Again and again Jesus pointed out that this was impossible. *"Either you are for me, or against me,"* He said. *"You cannot serve two masters at once. Either you hate one and love the other or vice-versa."* We are said elsewhere in Scripture (Rev. 3) to be hot or cold, zealous or callous. And here our Lord declares the same idea again. Either we are pungent, powerful people making a positive impact on our generation or we are lacking any potency except that of a negative, deadening influence.

Sad to say the charge frequently leveled against God's people by the world, that we are so "negative," is all too true. There are those who call themselves Christians who are such in name only. The potent powerful life of the risen Christ is not real in their experience. They know little or nothing about genuine godliness that makes a man or woman a force to be reckoned with in society. They do not produce the true, abundant fruits of the gracious Spirit of God.

Too often such people are not notable for the positive impact of their lives in any given community, but rather for the blight and barrenness of their behavior. Their speech, their attitudes, their entire deportment is such as to deaden everyone around them.

An experience I had on a flight from Nairobi to London many years ago will explain exactly what I mean. To save on travel expenses I booked a flight on a small, propeller-driven, charter aircraft of ancient vintage. It carried only

14 passengers, plus one stewardess in its erratic sort of bumpy, barn-storming flight over the great plains, mountains and deserts of the drowsy continent. Every hour or two we would set down at some remote, dusty, wind-swept airfield to drop off a few parcels or pick up a passenger from the bush.

We had not been airborne for very long before a wonderful spirit of good will, gaiety and camaraderie had developed among us as strangers. In fact I was able to have a most profitable and deep discussion with some of my seat mates about facing death as a Christian. I was being invalided back to Canada, with the medical prognosis that I had less than a month left to live.

In spite of the roaring, groaning engines, in spite of the bumpy flight in fierce air turbulence, in spite of the rickety plane which rattled so ominously, all of us were taking things in stride and making the best of a very rough flight.

We finally landed at Juba in the Sudan. There an austere, stern-faced, grimly dressed missionary lady from the Congo came aboard. In a loud voice and in no uncertain terms she promptly proceeded to let everyone know she had literally poured out her life for the poor Congolese.

Much more than that, however, from the moment she took her seat, she began to find fault with everything and everyone in that tightly packed aircraft. The seats were too narrow. The plane was too noisy. The pilot did not fly high enough. The flight attendant was not competent, even though the dear girl had performed wonders. The sandwiches served were stale. Her whole world was wrong.

The net result was to cast a pall and despair upon all those around her. Sitting so prim and proper in her self-preoccupation, her entire demeanor had a deadening impact on the other passengers. Her noxious, negative attitude destroyed the delightful, spontaneous good will that had engulfed us all before.

People began to mutter to one another. Cruel jests and cutting sarcasm were directed toward her.

And I for one felt flushed and ashamed to see the scorn and ridicule brought upon the character of Christ by one who claimed to be His follower.

Our lives, whether we are aware or not, either count for God or against Him. There simply is no middle ground. And the question which all of us must ask ourselves over and over is: "Does the life of Christ constitute the pungency, the power in my character?"

It is useless for us to attempt to do God's work in society unless the potency of our performance is the indwelling presence of the Spirit of God. To endeavor to make an impact on our generation apart from the awareness "Oh, God, it must be you who does it in me," our best efforts will be of no lasting consequence, no enduring benefit. The net result will be only a negative reaction, a deadening effect.

On the other hand, show me the man or woman in whom the presence of Christ is very real, very evident and that person's life will be positive for God. That is the individual who will supply strength for society, bring healing, instill enthusiasm, zest and good cheer; who will preserve the finest values, foster friendship and loyalty, and enter with redeeming love into the sadness and suffering of our sin-ridden society.

Looking back down the long, long trails of my own life I am deeply moved by remembering the men and women who were salt to me in such positive, helpful, wondrous ways. The touch of God's gracious Spirit upon my poor and often weary spirit came through the hands and hearts and homes of salty Christians. These were pungent people in whom the life of Christ was so apparent, so potent, so pure.

They were not phony play actors.

They were not false pretenders.

They were not professionals, putting on a performance.

I was oftentimes a wild, wayward and terribly strong-willed man not easily entreated. Yet in His own unique and generous way God used special, salty people to touch my life and turn me around.

I am deeply grateful to my Father in heaven that the presence of His own life was so obvious and manifest in these individuals, that He used them to draw me to Himself. As was said of the early apostles, "They had been with Jesus!" So I must say of those whose lives enriched my own.

In turn, testimony must be given to the fact that great good cheer comes to my own spirit when others tell of the way in which Christ has used my life or conduct as salt in their experience.

Several years ago a big, powerful, raw-boned rancher and his attractive wife came to call on us. They had both just committed their lives to Christ. We were the first people they wanted to tell the good news.

"Why did you come here first?" I asked in amazement. Their reply startled me. I could hardly believe it. "Because that hot blistering day you helped us harvest our crop and saved it from the terrible drought, we saw what it was like to be a Christian. And so we decided then, we would give our lives to God."

Out in the fierce summer sun of that rancher's fields, God had seen fit to use our simple labor and neighborly concern as a bit of salt that would bring this couple to Himself.

Today they travel all over the continent speaking, teaching, leading seminars in family life and counseling others who wish to come to Christ.

To be salt, we do not have to be spectacular.

To be salt, we do not have to be sensational.

To be salt, we do not have to be successful by the world's standards.

Rather, we have to be sensitive to the Spirit of God.

We have to be attuned to Christ's presence within us.

We have to be available to the purposes of God our Father for us and for others around us.

As we live and work and pray He will express His life through us as "salt for society." For He is not only our Savior, but also our savor of every good work and word in the world.